To F. T. H.
A brother in the order of nature
and in the order of grace.

# The
# CHURCH
## and
# SCIENCE

April 2, 1981, the Holy Father greets the
author at Plenary Session on "Science
and Unbelief."

# The
# CHURCH
# and
# SCIENCE

**By Most Reverend Mark J. Hurley**

**Preface by**
**Archbishop Paul Poupard**
**Pro-President, Secretariat for Non-Believers**

**ST. PAUL EDITIONS**

The texts of various pamphlets written by Bishop Hurley and published by the United States Catholic Conference are used herein through the kind permission of the United States Catholic Conference, copyright holder.

**Library of Congress Cataloging in Publication Data**
Hurley, Mark Joseph, 1917–
  The church and science.

  Bibliography
  1. Religion and science—1946—
BL240.2.H87     1982     261.5'5                                    I. Title.
                                                                    82-9955
                                                                    AACR2


ISBN  0-8198-1420-2 cloth
      0-8198-1421-0 paper

Printed in the U.S.A. by the Daughters of St. Paul
50 St. Paul's Ave., Boston MA 02130
The Daughters of St. Paul are an international community of religious women serving the Church with the communications media.

# CONTENTS

April 2, 1981, Pope John Paul greets
Archbishop Poupard, Pro-President, and
other members of the Secretariat for
Non-Believers.

# Preface

In our age, many young men and women, more than ever before, have been afforded the advantages of a systematic education that has opened their minds to a vast array of facts and notions about themselves and the physical world they live in. However, a characteristic of contemporary education is the stress on experiential knowledge and the scientific method of investigation and verification which is touted as the only legitimate way of attaining truth. It is an immanentistic stance that tends to reduce all reality to that which can be perceived by the senses, measured and quantified. In other words, it leaves no space for a reality that transcends the material cosmos, no space for investigating the primary cause and ultimate purpose of all created things. Generations have been brought up to regard scientific and religious views of reality as irreconcilable and mutually exclusive, or at most, as views of two distinct realities analogically defined: one objective, the other subjective.

Actually, at this point of scientific advancement, relatively few responsible scientists cling to that rationalistic position, and yet in the political arena, in many halls of learning and in the communications media, the irreconcilability of the two views is still a recurring cliché relied on to undermine the influence of religion or of Church authority wherever it conflicts with the power tactics of a particular party or ideology.

On the other hand, it is contended that the amazing pace of scientific discovery and technological sophistication, with all their undeniable benefits for the human race, has left theological reflection in the lee with many a question unanswered in terms of moral or ethical value judgments.

Bishop Mark Hurley of Santa Rosa, California, undertakes here to sort out these questions and to put them in their historical and contemporary context. It is with awe and trepidation that he looks at the "brave new world" wrought by scientific and technological progress. In a broad sweep he surveys what has been achieved in many areas of scientific research and assesses what it seems to portend.

In terms of achievement, science has immensely broadened our understanding of the universe, the macrocosm and the microcosm. It has devised techniques and instruments to probe the farthest reaches of outer space and the tiniest components of the atom. It has measured and harnessed nature's dynamic forces and bent them to the service of humanity, its needs, its comforts and also its ambitions, for better or for worse!

It has become clear that, in the process, scientists have acquired the power to tamper with nature's built-in balances and, in some memorable instances, have triggered mechanisms of wide-scale destruction. Today all eyes are fixed on the fingers which could trigger a world holocaust, and minds are searching wildly for a compelling force that could effectively stay such a dastardly impulse and insure our survival.

Apart from that extreme eventuality, there are many other areas in which science and technology are treading on dangerous ground. They have acquired the tools for wreaking irreparable mischief, and scientists themselves are afraid they may be unleashing monsters of their own making which they cannot control.

A fundamental need for our times is a truly human perspective that will take into account the meaning and purpose of human life, its origin and destiny which give it unique dignity and sacredness. Without this perspective nothing is secure, anything goes. The dimming of this perspective explains why it is that certain scientists pursue their goals regardless of the process which ultimately reduces human beings to the level of mere machines, to be "manufactured" according to specific standards for specific purposes, to be discarded if they are defective or unproductive.

Believers in God recognize the capacity and achievements of science; many have played significant roles in its advancement, but they also know that the human race cannot survive without a respect for the fundamental values of life. The judgment that moral reasoning has not kept pace with the rapid advances of science and technology has prompted Church leaders to foster a dialogue between religion and science. Many great scientists were and are indeed believers, but for some of them, their religious faith and their scientific knowledge belong to different levels of understanding and are not logically correlated. It is with a view to integrate and unify that which is perceived as separate and dissociated that the Catholic Church in particular has undertaken to foster dialogue with the world of science.

In the wake of Vatican Council II, Pope Paul VI established a Secretariat for Nonbelievers to which he entrusted the role, among others more explicitly indicated in its title, of facilitating contacts and dialogue with cultural groups which directly or indirectly contribute to alienation from religion or to religious indifference. Among these, of course, would be those which promote a so-called "scientific" materialism.

Since my own appointment in June 1980 to the pro-presidency of the Secretariat, Pope John Paul II has specifically requested that the Secretariat address itself to the relationships between faith and contemporary cultures in view of a better understanding and assessment of perceived cultural trends and attitudes.

Bishop Mark Hurley has been a Member of this Secretariat since 1974, and his contribution to its developments and efforts is deeply appreciated. As Chairman of the U.S. Bishops' Permanent Committee for Science, Technology and Human Values, he has done much to arouse concern over certain trends in the scientific and technological establishment which he and many other perceptive writers see as a very serious threat to human life and dignity. He has set himself a difficult task investigating many branches of scientific research and their relative techniques and goals.

In this volume, he is not attempting a complete exposé of what is amiss in the scientific enterprise and in its concept of progress, but he is giving voice to his deep concern and alerting his readers to the extremely grave consequences of a deliberate or witless disregard for essential human values. It is our hope and prayer that this voice will be heard and heeded.

ARCHBISHOP PAUL POUPARD
PRO-PRESIDENT
SECRETARIAT FOR NON-BELIEVERS

# Introduction

This book concerns itself with relationships.

The title *The Church and Science* is manifestly too broad and too vague. There is indeed a necessary and deep relationship between the Church and Science, but behind or within each there stands an army of scholars and popularizers, and, even more significantly, a vast multitude of human beings on this planet deeply affected by both. Theologians and philosophers seek value judgments on science and its achievements; scientists and technologists also seek value judgments but of a radically different nature. If Kipling's words are verified to the effect that "East is East and West is West, and Ne'er the twain shall meet," then the formula and scenario for disaster has come upon the human race.

The word "church" connotes much more than a mere organization and identifiable structure in the history of mankind. It signifies rather a "people," a people who adhere to and who support the Church and what it stands for. All people of one entire world have a fundamental stake in how the Church meets the modern world of science.

The word "science" also connotes much more than a national or international body of scientists and technologists. It too signifies a "people," not as well defined, perhaps, as a church, but yet a supporting public which ultimately approves and financially underwrites the progress of scientists and scientific organizations and structures both within and outside government.

Men, women and children over all the earth are constantly being exposed to the latest advances of science and technology. Not only are they exposed but often enough are made subjects, dependents, and even at time unwilling victims of the newest inventions. Perhaps even the word "intimidation" is not too strong in this context.

The public media of radio, television, and the press, often following the lead of scientists themselves, eagerly seize each new invention, each new discovery as "news," but just as often express extravagant claims and exaggerated projections of future import. With some justification, science has been touted as "the miracle worker," even as a sort of secular savior of the human race. The average man can scarcely be faulted if he responds in disappointment, disillusionment, and downright frustration as the new promised land, the new scientific utopia proves less than happy for him. Nor is the Church blameless in this result.

Writing in *Theological Studies* in December 1974, Richard A. Cipolla complained that: "The relationship between contemporary science and Christian dogmatic statements is one of the most neglected areas of contemporary theological thinking. We can only be amazed at the nearly complete silence of the theologians when confronted with the revolution of physics in the past fifty years....

"Much of the sterility of contemporary theology can be attributed to the fact that theologians have either completely ignored advances in physical sciences as somehow having nothing to do with them, or have been content to pick up a smattering of relativity theory from a popular magazine and allude to it in a most superficial manner...and let it go at that."

If the theologians can live in their ivory towers barely acknowledging the marvelous advances of science and technology, so too perhaps can the scientists be subject to the same unnatural dichotomy. The criticism, like a two-edged sword, might extend both ways.

Not only have scientists and technologists at times openly refused to acknowledge the patent relationships between their own discoveries and the application of them to the human race, but so many have asserted, in one form or another, that morality and ethics have no place with science by way of passing judgment on its actions and progress. Even further, as will be documented within, a significant number have responded that they are quite comfortable in maintaining a certain, almost radical, separation between themselves as scientists and themselves as members of the human race.

Their professional posture and their moral stance often run in parallel lines. Conscience and freedom of research and the application of research enjoy a very tenuous relationship at best and radical separation at worst.

Theologians, philosophers, scientists, and technocrats at times fain would enjoy a touch of schizophrenia in the most crucial areas of nuclear power, the genetic revolution, the computer revolution and a selected number of special topics with political ramifications. When one of the inventors of napalm, in response to a question of the morality of its use, can respond that he is "a scientist" and therefore neither moral nor immoral; that the use of napalm is of no concern to him as a scientist, then the picture is graphically drawn.

Nor is the general population exempt from blotting out of its consciousness the many life-and-death issues of modern society. Leaving moral judgments to scientists simply as scientists constitutes evasive action and a programmed amnesia.

Underlying all that is written herein lies the conviction that the Church must support all learning, all scholarship, all research but in a reasoned critical way. Furthermore, the Church must be seen to be in fact a patron of true progress in science and as a result in human affairs. L'Affaire Galileo, and the subsequent exploitation of it ever since down the centuries has placed the Church on the defensive all out of proportion to the significance of the event.

The Church has a vocation to act as the conscience of society, the Church as people perceiving the relationship between faith and reason, on the one hand, with science and applied technology on the other. It must take cognizance of the fact that pure, fundamental, and abstract science and the application of its discoveries concerns not only the men, women, and children of today, but future generations as well.

The purpose of this book is to point up some relationships which perforce come into being with the progress of both science and theology. Not only are there dozens of major problems not addressed, but no attempt is made to treat any problem in depth, not even the basic dignity of the human person and the concomitant right to life. While these and other values are clearly sustained, yet a much fuller and more sophisticated treatment must be sought elsewhere in theological, philosophical, and scientific literature.

Underlying this volume is the conviction that the Church can and must support all culture and civilization; must promote a true dialogue between theologians and philosophers and the scientists and technologists; and must do so without fear or hesitation. The Church sees God as the source of all truth. The Church understands that God cannot contradict Himself in His own creation, and not even in free human beings.

Pope John Paul II, on October 3, 1981, speaking to scientists, expressed his own personal confidence in scientists and science as an "integral part of culture." He added: "I have firm confidence in the world scientific community...and I am certain that...scientific research and its technical application will be carried out in full respect for the norms of morality, safeguarding human dignity, freedom, and equality.

"It is necessary that science should always be accompanied and controlled by the wisdom that belongs to the permanent spiritual heritage of humanity and that it takes its inspiration from the design of God implanted in creation...."

# CHAPTER ONE

## A NEW WORLD

> "Our age rejoices, and justly so, in the
> remarkable progress that has been
> made in scientific and philosophical
> knowledge."
> John XXIII, *Pacem in Terris*, no. 11

A new world is being born before the very eyes of the human race, a radically different age, different in every dimension. Yet this brave new world must needs answer the searching and inexorable challenge to the human race, namely, the value of human life itself. The question is fundamental.

With the cracking of the atomic code, man became capable of destroying life on earth on a scale undreamed of in his philosophies; with the cracking of the genetic code, man became capable of manipulating and controlling human nature itself. Both discoveries have empowered man to threaten his own dignity, his own freedom and his own very existence.

By the same token, supported by science and armed with technology, man has it within his power and grasp to protect and preserve life, to promote and enhance human dignity and human freedom.

Perhaps the portrait of mankind in this new age a-borning might well show *homo sapiens* cradling in his right hand the miracle drug penicillin to the glory of human life, and brandishing in his left hand a fusion hydrogen bomb to the consummation in holocaust of human life and its immolation on the altar of war. Man can indeed self-destruct. In the great game of life as it is lived on this planet, man is not only a player of the game, but also the cards that are played, and the stakes as well.

Scientists of varied disciplines—natural, life, behavioral, and social scientists; doctors of medicine and law; doctors of theology and philosophy; educators; administrators of health services; politicians; military experts and interested citizens: all can contribute to a consensus that mankind must arrive at. No one person, no one group, no one scientific discipline can provide the answers. Solutions, like truth itself, will be complex, sophisticated and inter-disciplinary, for there is no scientific Utopia on earth nor a religious Utopia, either. Such is the case precisely because men, women, and children are by nature pilgrims seeking answers, insights and wisdom in relation to nature's deepest mystery and most elusive secret: the gift of life.

In another context, what happens to man, to human life, to human values in an autonomous technological society? Where science meets the human person, what is the result?

The science-fiction novel, *Fail-Safe,* describes man as feeling "helpless" in an autonomous technological society. Initially, he seeks relief from drudgery and the slavery of hard and monotonous labor through technology and mechanical devices; then he seeks relief from the drudgery of and slavery to the very machines invented to liberate him. Moreover, he feels helpless as the all-powerful state, armed by science and technology, breeds impersonal monsters that know how to control, how to destroy, but not how to liberate and cure. The book asks an ultimate question: "Has man himself become obsolete?"

Such, however, is not the Christian message, which is one of hope, which envisions a true symbiosis between science and mankind wherein two seemingly disparate things learn to live together in mutual harmony to mutual advantage. This message of rising expectations affirms that "the age of technology is part of the great and mysterious evolution of the universe devised by God...(for the) taking over of the planet by mankind." (Ong)

One of the principal precincts wherein science and mankind meet in the field of health care and its primary theater is the hospital. Where the cold, hard steel of technology touches the warm, soft flesh of the human person there necessarily arises a whole myriad of problems—human, ethical, moral, spiritual—problems and dilemmas of a most sophisticated and complicated nature that admit of no easy solutions. Hence, the urgent and pressing need for clear thinking and prayerful reflection on the part of all concerned, but especially the scientists, the doctors of medicine, the philosophers and the theologians.

The problems are almost without end. Some concern life itself and its dignity: abortion, contraception, sterilization, experimentation on human beings, euthanasia and suicide; others are connected with genetics: amniocentesis, genetic screening, genetic engineering, *in vitro* fertilization and test-tube babies. There is the matter of what patient gets access to the sophisticated, complicated and expensive equipment; who receives the heart transplant, the cornea, the kidney; who gets access to the dialysis machine? There is the problem of privacy and the threatened invasion of professional and medical secrets, particularly through the use of computers and data banks; there is the matter of free, informed consent to operations and experimentation. These and many more problems demand the very best intelligence and moral balance that a nation is capable of.

Men and women of science are not unaware of moral dimensions.

On September 4, 1974, with the headline, "Scientists Fear Genetic Plague," the story, datelined in London, told how influential scientists were expressing increasing alarm about the danger of genetic experiments which might unleash a global plague as perilous to mankind as nuclear war. For perhaps the first time in history, the biologists prodded the National Academy of Sciences in the United States to urge scientists everywhere to halt work on genetic engineering until such time as the character of the experiments in genetics could be determined. The president for The British Association for the Advancement of Science asserted that experiments could accidentally touch off a sharp increase in disease, e.g., of cancer in the world, precisely because new techniques have been discovered for the isolation and the rejoining of segments of DNA. In other words, bacteria can be made to exchange genetic information, the result being bacteria pathogenic to man and harmful to all life systems for which science at present has no antidotes.

Similarly the Hollywood movie called "The Andromeda Strain," a science-fiction piece, suggested that some kind of disease could come in from outer space. "The Andromeda Strain" was simply science-fiction, but the transfer of genetic information from one bacteria to another could soon involve an experimental procedure which, in the words of one eminent biologist, "could be done by any high school student."

Significantly, even the scientific community issued warnings that there must be some kind of moral judgment made as to the value or the dangers of uncontrolled experimentation. Or perhaps it should be said that scientists, too, have recognized values over and above experimentation itself, that experiments are not ends in themselves, and that science does not bring its own moral values.

Such is but one illustration among thousands which support the thesis that a new world is being born before the very eyes of the human race.

By uncovering the secrets of the genetic code, man has made himself capable of controlling and manipulating man in a new dictatorship of tyranny and control through biological engineering. The right to life, the quality of life, control of life, human freedom and human dignity, all weigh in the balance in this brave new world.

Technology, too, with electronic achievements, has brought an unheard of skill in the surveillance of man by fellow man: wire taps and listening devices, computers and data banks, threaten to invade man's right to privacy, to erode his right to be left alone. Big brother looms large on the horizon, and he is not a product of science-fiction.

But as ominous a threat as this brave new world of science and technology is, yet it is, at the same time, a world of great promise and almost infinite opportunity. The harnessing of space outside man, the mastering of space inside of man, offer maximum potential for the improvement of living conditions;

the care and cure of the sick and handicapped; the lightening of oppressive physical labor—in a word, for the happiness of man on this mortal coil.

But the key issue in this brave new world is not science or technology as such, but what values men will live by and have their being. With the increasing secularization of man wherein the question is not, "How does a man live in a society which does not acknowledge God?" but, rather, "How does he live in a society wherein so many false gods are worshipped?" In the much-quoted best seller, *Future Shock* (p. 179), the author put his finger deftly on the central issue; he asserted that "ultimately the problems are not scientific or technical but ethical and political. Choice—the criteria of choice—will be crucial."

This new world promises to bring an end to the traditional Christendom of past centuries—a world in which society was still based on the Judeo-Christian understanding of reality. It will not mean the end of Christianity, much less of the need for Christ and His message. But the human values and the basic moral principles of the Judeo-Christian tradition, once assumed as "in possession," accepted on all sides as basic to modern society and American civilization, once the agreed consensus of public opinion, the underpinning of the Declaration of Independence, have been overturned and deeply eroded. Even the certain inalienable rights endowed by the Creator—the right to life, liberty, and the pursuit of happiness—cannot be reckoned as accepted and revered by the vast majority, precisely because basic values have come into question, especially under the new and awesome powers that have been placed in the hands of the modern man—it's a new world!

The increased autonomy of the secular, however, does not spell the end of religion or religious concerns; while the religious dimension still holds the 20th century man's interest, yet he is often restive and alienated in his new world. He finds himself submerged, in the USA, in material abundance and technical achievement, a prodigious consumer of goods and services, to the detriment of the true depth of his being and the quality of his life. While he admires "science," he sees no scientific Utopia as promised, and hence lives in doubt and uncertainty. Many people are asking the religious question: the nature of God and man, of life and death. Some, however, who seem not to have even an obscure consciousness of the existence of God, yet are convinced in the light of the history of the 20th century, perhaps the most bloody century on record, that science of itself cannot bring happiness. Nor is such a conclusion surprising.

The uses of science and technology are always moral and political questions, never simply scientific or technical. Inevitably, "to do or not to do," "to experiment or not to experiment," involve judgments about values. These value judgments, even if made by scientists, do not derive from science as such.

Leon R. Kass in *Science*, Nov. 1971, gave some of the reasons for this conclusion, which reasons "are often overlooked." Scientists like to talk of "the control of nature by science," but it is men who control. Science may give the means but "men choose the ends; the choice of ends comes from beyond science.

"The ancients conceived of science as the understanding of nature, pursued for its own sake. We moderns view science as power, as control over nature, the conquest of nature...."

Clearly, then, there is ample room for abuse of power—dependent, of course, on values chosen, consciously or unconsciously.

Science, accordingly, does not bring with it built-in values for human behavior. Rather it does often have a bias in the exaltation of the quantitative over the qualitative, the objective over the subjective. As science reveals more and more wondrous things, it always comes to the revelation of yet new and further mysteries. Each new advance brings further mystery and raises the question: is there any meaning beyond this mystery?

The United States of America is moving toward a eugenic society wherein perfection seems to lie in the possession of a perfect set of chromosomes and genes. The drive to eliminate the "defectives" has taken on mammoth proportions; bioethics has become a by-word, but often a word without true ethical or moral religious roots. The drive to control and manipulate man is no myth; it moves on relentlessly in its mechanistic view of man. Carl Sagan, the "glamour boy" of scientists turned celebrity, asserted in his best seller *Cosmos* that man is a machine.

In the United States it can fairly and justly be affirmed that both the legal and medical professions, by and large as bodies, have abdicated their responsibilities in the question of right to life, the right to kill. Most influential in promoting abortion on demand was, over the years, the American Bar Association's *Model Penal Code.* Similarly, during the 1960's, medical school after medical school quietly repudiated the Hippocratic Oath, its treatment of both abortion and euthanasia, by deleting it from the traditional place in the graduation ceremonies of the newly-degreed doctors of medicine.

The poor, the aged, the sick, the insane, the desperately ill, the defectives, the racially different—those without that set of perfect chromosomes—beware! The traditional protections have been eroded in the name of science and humanity. Joseph Fletcher, the prophet of "situation ethics," may well be cited to illustrate: "If we are morally obligated to put an end to a pregnancy when amniocentisis reveals a terribly defective fetus, we are equally obliged to put an end to a patient's hopeless misery...."

It is proxy judgment! Big brother knows best!

Large segments of major forces in the United States, including, for example, the National Academy of Sciences, are committed to a planned eugenic society. And this new society, fashioned along the specifications of science and technology, unrestrained by and alienated from truly human and humane considerations, will be essentially and inherently anti-Christian and anti-human. There is arising a secular answer which denies basic human dignity and freedom. It is the end of Christendom but the beginning of a new call for the message of Christ.

Is it any wonder that modern man is so restive in his brave new world?

# CHAPTER TWO

## THE CHURCH'S ANSWER
## MUST BE DIFFERENT

> "For recent studies and findings
> of science, history, and philosophy
> raise new questions which influence
> life and demand new theological inves-
> tigations."
>
> Vatican II, *Gaudium et Spes*, no. 62

The Church looks to affirm not only that God is not dead or irrelevant, but that God lives and is faithful. The Church demonstrates that it too lives and is faithful in spite of adverse currents of history on the children of science in any age or epoch. The Church proclaims the dignity of man in the Incarnation and the brotherhood of man in nature because of his creation by God.

The Church as well faces a great opportunity to penetrate the new insights into man and creation; to cooperate with scientists, making clear its disinterested concern for man, for his progress, and for him yet further to become master of the mysteries of the natural world. The Church expresses its belief that it never fears science or technology, and sees neither as necessary threats to revealed religion, precisely because the Church believes in the unity of all truth, God being its source.

Science and technology, in turn, need the moral experience and ethical intuition of the Church. The ongoing destruction of defective men by other men, the fabrication of men by other men, the domestication of men by other men, the invasion of man and his private life by reduction to a specific number by other men, challenge not simply ethical principles, but the deepest dogmatic and doctrinal truths.

The conception that science is an independent body of knowledge, coldly objective, without any cultural bias of its very own; that science is a means par excellence of conquering social problems and creating a Utopia on earth through inevitable evolution and progress, is itself a cultural bias.

There is, moreover, a breakdown of communications between laymen and scientists. The general public often accepts scientific authority with blind reverence, almost religious in nature. Scientists, in turn, often reject the unifying philosophical themes, the underlying human value in their research, ignoring the social consequences of their ideas. Nor should it be thought that scientists are always optimistic about the future.

Just a few years ago, the famous anthropologist, L.S.B. Leakey, who had labeled the Peking man as being 100,000 years old, attended a press conference in San Francisco in conjunction with a symposium on his colleague, Father Teilhard de Chardin. Professor Leakey had just lately discovered the Tanganyika man, which he asserted was 300,000 years old. The reporters asked him how long man had been upon earth, and Leakey said that he estimated that man probably went back some 20 million years. Then he was asked about the future of the human race.

His dolorous replies pointed out that man had discovered atomic energy, and, with it, bombs, biological warfare and chemical warfare, and that man was making for himself not milestones of civilization, but tombstones. He predicted slavery by 1984, by reason of both the use of drugs and bio-engineering. He cried out that "where faith is maimed, science is blind." His faith was, he said, that man could be perfectible and could literally become God, but instead he saw nothing but doom; tombstones, instead of milestones of civilization.

The reporters were very upset by this somber forecast and over and over asked could they not get a word of hope, a tiny ray of hope from the great professor. Finally, he relented and said, well maybe man could come to a higher consciousness and come to his senses. And then he was asked:

"Well, how long do you think that would take?" And his answer was: "Twenty million years more."

Similarly, no one could listen to Professor Schockley of Stanford University, Nobel prize winner for his invention of the transistor, explaining his theories on racial inferiority and not hear a social engineer propagating his narrow prejudices outside his field of competence.

These examples, among hundreds more, serve to illustrate a cultural bias; a set of moral values, and, indeed, say a great deal about trust or the lack of trust in the providence of God.

The Church recognizes that scientists have their own competences. The Church welcomes the advance and progress of science and technology but at the same time refuses to baptize and accept every change as it occurs. The new world is not to be opposed automatically, nor believers isolated in a religious ghetto from it. Catholics must stand in the mainstream of human life. But it is a necessary function to judge change from a moral and ethical vantage point. The Church rejects modernism as a heresy of surrender, which has "seen the human face of the Church but has misconceived her divine nature" (Suhard). At the same time, it rejects integralism, the heresy which makes the Church, because of its transcendence, an out-of-this-world or other-worldly community divorced from God's own creation, divorced from history, divorced from the Incarnation. The Church's role is to save the world, not to conquer it.

If, in the words of Pope Pius XII, "We believe that the moral history of a nation is more important than its scientific history," then it seems so obvious to conclude that the message of the Church and its people, the message of Catholics, must indeed be different. But, different from what? What difference the message of Christ in this brave new world?

The French proverb says that "the more things change, the more they are the same." Change indeed presupposes something permanent, some continuity with the past. Thus the message of Christ is both conservative of the past yet different today, different as to time, to persons, to the solution of problems, and even purposes.

Timeless yet different in time, Christ's living message grows and increases to meet new challenges. It is the Church's duty at once to preserve the deposit of faith and revelation, and also to interpret it authoritatively, setting forth its content in each epoch of history, in every nation, and to every creature. The brave new world, in its historical and cultural realities; its challenges of the atomic age; its marvels of the genetic age; its successes of the technological age, meets the message of Christ suited to these times.

Believers in God and transcendent man, American Catholics in particular and those espousing the message of Christ, find themselves once again in a new minority status in the USA, for example. No longer does the message of Christendom find a majority consensus; no longer are the Judeo-Christian values of the past "in possession" but, on the contrary, are being eroded and destroyed. American Catholics are once again being forced into the position of dissenters from the majority consensus precisely because their message is different.

Once again America's dissenting minority is more and more being labeled "Catholic."

The attack on family life from many sides perhaps best illustrates what is happening.

The legal profession through the American Bar Association, in promoting its model penal code in the 1950's with its decriminalization of procured abortion, laid the legislative and judicial groundwork for the denial of the right to life. When the medical profession was faced with the ancient, time-honored, and traditional Hippocratic Oath with its strictures against induced abortion and direct euthanasia; when it realized that this Oath given at the graduation of physicians and surgeons from medical schools stood in direct contradiction to the "new ethics," it did not bother to refute the ancient wisdom but simply abolished the taking of the Oath.

The U.S. Supreme Court then canonized the position in its 1973 decision which sanctioned virtual abortion-on-demand.

In spite of the protestations of the Chief Justice Burger that the decision was not "abortion-on-demand," subsequent results proved him in error. The "restrictions" which evolved are so minor and so easily by-passed as to be nugatory. Justice White's assessment that the decision was an exercise in raw judicial power stands as the more prophetic.

It should be underscored that science and technology were invoked to buttress these radical deviations from the traditional Judeo-Christian and other moral and ethical precedents. The results in education have been all but disastrous; the young are being educated in a new ambience.

The state schools may now teach what many consider an abomination: abortion-on-demand, sterilization, contraception, and other allied matters, as constitutional rights. Some teach these practices as civic duty and moral obligation.

The most honored and revered Rabbi Abraham Heschel asserted that "secular schools have failed. They have failed on a variety of levels.... (They) give plenty of information, food for the mind, but do nothing about training of the emotions, do nothing about training of the will.... The American educational system on all levels has proved to be a terrible disappointment."

"Religious schools?...I only wish I could tell you that religious schools are doing a perfect job. I would say the religious schools deserve some (government) support because they are doing partly a good job. They at least teach people some of the great classical ideas of the religious tradition. Take away religious tradition and what is left?" (Feb. 4, 1973, NBC/TV Network)

Little wonder that the family is threatened, the parents fearful, the children intimidated! Often in the name of the new discoveries of science which makes these things possible!

And similarly down through a list of problems and their solutions in this new world: racial discrimination; ecology; population; rights of farmworkers; sensitivity training; the invasion of privacy; war and weapons; foreign aid. These problems all share in common. Solutions and answers deviate from the general consensus in so many instances. So be it!

American Catholics do not wish to deviate from the norm just to be different. Nor do they seek sectarian victory or partisan advantage. Rather, they have a very positive, optimistic view of man, of life, of mystery, and of the meaning of it all under God. The Declaration of Independence put it so well that rights are God-given and include the right to life and liberty. The purposes of the Church are not, and must never be, self-seeking or self-serving.

The Church, which is people basically, sees all men as made to the image and likeness of God. It sounds almost sacrilegious precisely because the first commandment of the Old Law forbade graven images of God.

It sees man not only as a creature with needs like the animals, who also have needs, but as having goals in this life and the next; man as transcendent precisely because of the mystery of the Incarnation wherein Jesus Christ ennobled human nature.

It respects nature and its secrets; scientists and technocrats, discovering and using these secrets as instruments in the Divine Plan, as allies not as enemies, in the Providence of God.

It recognizes God working in all human history.

It accepts the Sermon on the Mount as a moral norm and human nature as essentially good, in need of care and the grace of God.

With 2,000 years of tradition, with centuries of social tradition, of family tradition, often substantially different from that of neighbors, yet it offers its cooperation in the temporal and spiritual welfare of all.

Consequently, Catholics affirm that the struggle is worth it; indeed, the struggle for justice and charity in our land is a categorical imperative; and the faithful rejoice that they have been born to affirm the message of Christ to a world that needs it so desperately.

Their purpose in a nutshell is not to conquer anyone but to bring the message, so different, to each of their neighbors, convinced that he will know the truth and the truth will make him free in the brave new world of science and technology.

# CHAPTER THREE

## IS LIFE CHEAP IN THE WORLD?

> "There is no man, no human
> authority, no science, no medical,
> eugenic, social, economic or moral
> 'indication' that can offer òr produce
> a valid juridical title to a direct
> deliberate disposal of an innocent
> human life."
>
> Pius XII, *Allocution to Midwives,*
> October 29, 1951

What premium, what value are Americans and others placing on human life? Has there been a serious erosion in our society, a fundamental depreciation in the perception and understanding of God's gift of life? The evidence seems quite conclusive that life is becoming cheap and expendable.

There hangs over the entire earth the sword of Damocles, more properly called war and warfare, abetted and changed radically by the new science and the new technology. And what are the ABC's of warfare? "A" stands for atomic, which promises fusion bombs annihilating major portions of the world's population in a twinkling. The November, 1976, *Scientific American* assesses that 18 million in the USA will die in a "first strike" of atomic bombs from enemy attack; some 60 million casualties will follow as well. No estimate is given for subsequent events but it is clear that mankind will seek shelter underground and in caves, a throw-back to early pre-history.

"B" stands for biological, which promises exotic weapons which will unleash killer Andromeda strains, hybrid organisms begetting plagues and scourges, made possible, perhaps, by the newly discovered recombinant qualities of the molecule DNA. "C" signifies chemical, which presages noxious and lethal gases, more effective napalm, fiery and pyrotechnic compounds that kill on contact.

The ABC's of warfare do say something about science and technology, and, more, about the value of life on the planet earth.

Violence and terror, especially in larger cities, have become a veritable way of life all over the globe, and a method in the solution of human problems. But not only is violence to be found on the streets, it is actually featured and glorified on the television screens across the land. And violence is almost always against human life. The Mayor of San Francisco, who told its citizenry that there were no longer any neighborhoods that were safe because of random and senseless violence, himself died shortly thereafter at the hands of an assassin.

The list of famous leaders who were victims of assassins' bullets or attempts on their lives names almost all the world leaders. Whether President Kennedy or his brother Robert, Martin Luther King, Aldo Moro, Ghandi, Archbishop Romero or those who escaped death like DeGaulle, Roosevelt, Truman, Ford, Reagan or Pope John Paul II, the education in violence moves on apace and reflects society's estimation of human values and the value of life.

Abortion, another form of violence practiced in modern society and on all continents, in such a very short space of time has indeed constituted a revolution against the judgment of generations. While experts carry on learned debates about unusual cases such as those resulting from rape or incest, of those concerning the unborn with mental defects or Tay-Sachs disease or the Down syndrome and the like, over a million healthy, normal unborn babies in the USA alone each year are destroyed on demand. And thanks to amniocentesis and genetic screening, some are destroyed precisely because they are not of the desired sex. This balancing of the convenience of the mother as weighed against the value of life, this philosophy of expediency certainly has something to say about the value of life in any country. It has brought about, at the very least, the derogation—if not the abrogation—of the Hippocratic Oath in medical schools, and the loss of its protection of life to society at large.

Even the aborted fetuses have become "fair game" for the scientists. Some fetuses live for hours after abortion; they often can be kept alive for a time. Under the Supreme Court decision they have in practice absolutely no rights at all. One scientist has put the matter very clearly: even animals have more rights in the experimental laboratory, precisely because the people who are sending the money, like the foundations, specify the rules under which the experimentations can be performed on animals.

Why is this such an important thing to so many scientists? The answer is that these aborted fetuses represent a treasure trove. They are gold in the hills; tissues, hearts and lungs and bones and all the rest that are there to be used for transplants—there to be used, as they say, perhaps in the cure of cancer. This fresh tissue is appropriated in the name of future generations. And again the proxy judgment is made. The argument runs thusly: if this little defective child really could give an informed consent, it is sure that the child itself would offer to sacrifice its life for the life of children in the ages to come. So again the proxy judgment.

Decisions are being made for the poor, the crippled, the retarded, the unborn, etc., who really are not usually in a position to give informed, full consent. The "new" morality, in other words, dictates that there is an obligation, in charity, to give up life, to lay down one's life for friends, whereas it should be talking justice, and consequently, informed consent. This judgment of obligation "in charity" almost always falls upon the weak, rarely on the strong. People do not put such obligations on themselves.

Meanwhile, the proponents of outright infanticide, the killing of infants, have been making their voices heard in the public forum. Academic philosophers are saying, with reason and, indeed, the logic upon which they pride themselves, that there is no essential difference between abortion and infanticide. It is not surprising, then, to read in a philosophical journal an article by philosopher Michael Tooley, for example, suggesting that infants who do not meet certain standards also be destroyed for the sake of society. There was also a symposium in the making with the title, "Permissible and Disputed Means of Infanticide." Nobel laureate and scientist James Watson has suggested that babies be allowed birth, only to be declared legally alive or dead after three days. So much for some philosophers on the value of life!

Society faces many challenges and problems in reference to the mentally ill, the mentally retarded, the old, the poor, the incurably diseased. Presumably from the field of economics comes a new moral criterion known as the "cost-benefit" theory. It says, in essence, that when a person becomes too expensive to maintain in our society, it is time that he be dispatched to eternal glory. The more important matter here is, the question of who decides. Is it Big Brother? Who gives the proxy consent? Who says what value a specific life has? What judge affirms that there is worthless life or that life in any form lacks meaning? Is it the state who is Big Brother?

California hospitals for the mentally ill, as well as prison hospitals, have been constantly under intensive inquiry for several years because of a suspicion of forced medication and, indeed, too many deaths and too many unexplained practices. The question of death and dying, of course, is not easily answered, but how it is solved, and by whom, says very much about the value of life in society.

And, finally, there are the simple news items that come day by day, that tell so much about the value of a human being in society. On November 10, 1976, in San Francisco, for example, a motorist was convicted in the death of eight people. His penalty was a $300 fine. Another man was convicted of killing a dog; his penalty, one year in jail. Almost every day the public is asked to read and contribute to campaigns and crusades to save the whales, to save the porpoises off the coasts. Over the national news a bulletin went out warning hunters in Texas that they may kill the gray cranes, but that the white whooping crane is mixing with the gray ones, and, if they are shot or killed, there will be a fine of $10,000 and a prison term as well. At the same time a United States senator was vehemently protesting the sterilization by the United

States Government of some 3,000 Indian women by its own health service, the implication being that informed consent was almost never obtained or, in many cases, even possible.

The recitation of this litany against life and limb might remind one of a classic Greek drama of Aeschylus or of Sophocles: first, the servant is killed; then the beloved daughter of the king is murdered; next, the beloved younger son is poisoned; then, the eldest son, it is reported, is killed in battle, followed by the suicide of the queen and, finally, the king plunges off the walls of the fortress in utter despair and agony. And the play is over because everyone is dead. There is another side to this litany.

Mankind must not forget—indeed, the Church wishes to emphasize—that men and women of science and technology have undertaken heroic measures to preserve, protect and enhance life and human dignity. It is not just to indict the whole of society, or even a majority of its members, or of scientists, in their concern for justice and human dignity.

However, a nation cannot be satisfied that a majority of its people are not mugged or murdered in the streets; that bombs, even fusion bombs, will not kill every single person in the world; that in most areas, although not in two of the USA's largest cities, children coming to term alive outnumber those who are the victims of abortion, and that elderly people are indeed in good health and happy. The point is that, just as freedom is whole and entire, just as human dignity is indivisible, just as liberty must be for all and not just for a few or for a class, so, too, when one life, much less when whole categories of human life in our society are unjustly threatened, then all are.

Life, freedom and human dignity are being devaluated in our society.

Dr. Leon Kass, the eminent biologist from the University of Chicago, pointed to the high price mankind is paying for its unrestrained conquest of nature and ruthless exploitation of the environment. The ecology crisis was foreseen and ignored until serious damage forced redress. Then he added, "With the powers for biological engineering now gathering, there will be splendid new opportunities for a similar degradation of our view of man. Indeed, we are already witnessing the erosion of our idea of man as something splendid or divine, as a creature with freedom and dignity. Clearly, if we come to see ourselves as meat, meat we shall be."

It is not science or technology that threatens, but man himself with his finger on the atomic button, or his Saturday-night special in his pocket, or his deadly dose of drugs, or even his denial of economic justice. Man's conscience which must judge right from wrong, man himself who is the player of the cards, the cards themselves, and the very stakes being played for.

More and more the concept of "the quality of life" is being offered to supersede "the right to life." When a human being becomes, or is perceived as becoming only a function of society, or the earth, or cosmos, or in a void where there is no God or the recognition of the transcendental in man, then there follows the complete erosion of the value of life.

In a dehumanized, secularized world where God is not acknowledged, and precisely because it does not acknowledge the transcendent God, it worships many false gods, to the peril of life and liberty.

# CHAPTER FOUR

## SOME RELATIONSHIPS
## OF SCIENCE AND RELIGION
## IN THE GENETIC REVOLUTION

> "Wake up, man, and recognize the high
> estate of your human nature.
> Remember you are made in God's
> image...."
>
> Pope St. Leo the Great (461)

The more burning questions of the modern era call for value judgments made by theologians and philosophers; by scientists themselves as human beings concerned with the effects of their works; legislators and judges; and by the general public, who must live by the decisions made. Science, as has been pointed out already, does not generate its own values, much less human values. Yet value judgments are not always easily made. The genetic revolution illustrates the necessity for interdisciplinary collaboration and cooperation in the interests of the human race.

The remarkable and dramatic discovery of deoxyribonucleic acid, DNA; the fierce public debate on the taking of human life *in utero;* the advent of the first test-tube baby, charmingly welcomed into this world by Pope John Paul I while he questioned the morality of the means employed; and the rising tide in favor of "death with dignity," "mercy killing" and other euphemisms covering the stark word "euthanasia"; and the patenting of new life forms are urgent problems in modern society, on all continents, and seemingly for all times.

## Recombinant DNA Research

Recombinant DNA research is an issue which illustrates the endeavor of scientists and the public to ensure scientific progress in a fashion that respects human values. This debate has not yet come to full maturity; it is too early to determine precisely how to reconcile scientific inquiry, public health, human values, and policy in this matter. It is not too early, however, to outline its many dimensions and to urge informed public participation.

Since the question of recombinant DNA is a paradigm of other scientific issues involving values and public policy dimensions, the approach in this instance will be normative of the way these other matters are handled.

There are moral dimensions beyond the hazards issue; and some guidelines in moral reasoning concerning recombinant DNA research are essential for true progress.

## History

The modern era of molecular biology began almost thirty years ago with the identification of DNA as the chemical basis of heredity and the discovery of its general structure. Advances in molecular biology now permit the joining of portions of DNA molecules from different species into "DNA recombinants," which are then inserted into bacterial cells. This technique will facilitate increased knowledge of basic biological processes because it makes possible the study of individual genes and their component parts.

Recombinant DNA research has already increased understanding of the organization of genes in lower organisms and of gene duplication. It is rightly thought that there will be almost unlimited beneficial practical applications as well. On the other hand, the research is a cause of concern because some experiments may pose new, unanticipated risks. Biologists are altering the genes of living things without being able to predict the outcome.

Because this technology has the potential to modify all forms of life, it requires full exploration of the ends it serves and the means to these ends. Serious, thoughtful reflection on these matters as well as responsible collaboration between scientists and the public are morally and pragmatically imperative. This process of reflection was initiated by the scientific community on an international level and has expanded to include members of the public in some local communities. The nature and extent of the debate calls for respectful, patient, responsible behavior on the part of all participants.

Simply stated, the dilemma is this: investigation involving recombinant DNA promises great theoretical advances. Moreover, this technique will have practical applications (e.g., in medicine and agriculture). At the same time, because the research is new (in some cases involving pathogenic substances and sometimes new organisms) it may involve unknown and potentially grave risks. It is generally agreed that there is need for caution since DNA molecules could escape from the laboratory with consequences which cannot be foreseen. Parties to the controversy adopt various stances ranging from the opinion that already too much time has been lost and work should proceed apace, to the other extreme which would ban all recombinant DNA research as inherently too risky.

## Controlling the Genie

Without detailing the history of the entire controversy, several commendable aspects of the debate should be noted. The issue came to public attention through the responsible action of scientists themselves who were concerned about the possible hazards. Furthermore, molecular biologists voluntarily imposed a moratorium on the conduct of certain types of recombinant DNA research while the situation was reviewed. The process of deliberation about the technique and its hazards was opened. In other words, there has been a serious effort on the part of some scientists to consider the risk dimension of the matter.

In June 1976, a year-long discussion of safeguards resulted in the publication of guidelines by the National Institutes of Health which specify how grantees of NIH must conduct recombinant DNA research. These guidelines stipulate two types of containment: physical and biological. The physical containment requirements are designed to confine organisms containing recombinant DNA to the laboratory. The biological containment requirements stipulate the use of weakened strains of host cells, so that, should any organisms escape from physical containment, they could not survive. Agreement is lacking, however, on the adequacy of the guidelines to prevent such an occurrence. The guidelines do not apply to industrial and other private research not funded by the government.

Proponents of recombinant DNA research cite its potential benefits (e.g., the development of new methods for understanding and controlling disease, the synthesis of interferon and insulin) and the adequacy of the NIH guidelines to prevent any undesirable consequences, which, they contend, are at this point merely hypothetical. Critics of the technique tend to focus on the potential for health hazards (e.g., novel and uncontrollable epidemics) and on the unknown and lasting effects of such intervention in the evolutionary process; the censuring in 1981 of Dr. Cline of UCLA for unauthorized experiments in DNA.

There are basic ethical questions about recombinant DNA research which should be raised and dispassionately addressed. Have scientists sufficiently investigated the potential for hazard to justify this research? To exercise a moderating influence on recombinant DNA studies, does one need to identify or only suspect substantial risk? Who should judge the acceptability of risk? Has there been sufficiently wide dissemination of balanced, accurate information about recombinant DNA for the public to contribute intelligently to policy-making in this regard? Are the NIH guidelines adequate? Can they be enforced, and if so, how? Is legislation a satisfactory way of managing or controlling this research? What is the responsibility of the United States on an international level in dealing with recombinant DNA? Is recombinant DNA only a prelude to more extensive genetic modification, i.e., to human engineering? How far does the public want to advance in genetic engineering in the eventual fabrication of man?

The controversy surrounding these techniques highlights the issue of freedom of scientific inquiry and the role of the public in science policy. Among the values prized by the scientific community are, understandably, scientific knowledge and the freedom to pursue it. With these as with all values, however, the potential exists for conflict with other human values. Knowledge gained in recombinant DNA research ought not be at the expense of other fundamental values. Because the well-being and health of human and other forms of life may be at stake, concerned persons should become involved in the dialogue.

At stake is the question of precisely how to balance the value of scientific inquiry with responsibility to humanity at large. It seems wise, however, to inject a note of caution and prudence in the awesome task of so doing.

## Role of the Public

A fundamental issue in this debate concerns the public's relationship to scientific research. *Contrary to the notion of value-free science, almost every scientific endeavor has transcientific dimensions—dimensions which pertain to aspects of human life other than the scientific.* These dimensions involve ethical and public policy implications. In keeping with the right of self-determination, the public should know about scientific research and be able to judge for itself the acceptability of the risk which such experimentation entails for present and future generations. Furthermore, if the discussion includes an informed public, the debate is likely to consider more than the specific issue of biohazards. The focus may expand from the means of achieving greater knowledge to include the end or goal of the activity. A multi-disciplinary effort should consider the social, political, economic, and ethical implications of such research. Reflection is called for on the meaning of the direction microbiology is taking in recombinant DNA research.

## Moral Dimension

The Church, while recognizing its limitations in scientific matters, has something to contribute to this reflection. The *Pastoral Constitution on the Church in the Modern World* observes that "recent research and discoveries in the sciences, in history and philosophy bring up new problems which have an important *bearing on life* itself and demand new scrutiny by theologians." In other words, the new circumstances which challenge traditional understandings of human values must be met with creativity and imagination, reflecting a fuller and deeper understanding of the values at stake.

Yet, in this era of unprecedented scientific capabilities the pursuit of knowledge or truth is not the sole criterion for responsible scientific inquiry, especially in light of the limitations of our human condition. A desire to control the totality of life, coupled with increased technological might, produces an inflated sense of autonomy and tends to obscure the fact that man's intelligence and creativity are limited. There is more to reality than what is subject to scientific investigation and manipulation. *Each scientific advance does not necessarily constitute real human progress.* This realization should suggest a pause before the human race pursues everything which is scientifically feasible. Wisdom is also necessary if the good of humankind is really to be achieved.

The fundamental moral imperative is that good is to be pursued and evil to be avoided. People are strictly obliged to avoid harm, but are not obliged to accomplish all "good." It is possible to harm future generations by negligently omitting to accomplish some things via science. On the other hand, mankind is not obliged to accomplish everything possible through science at whatever risk or at the price of assaulting time-honored values. Christians and others have always refused to vest *absolute* value in any human good or endeavor. The technological imperative that, "All that can be done, must be done" may well prove both immoral and disastrous.

In determining what should be done, man must be wary of a strictly utilitarian mode of reasoning and not look only to consequences. Actions must not only point to or produce future goods. They must also respect and reflect the range of *human* goods in the process. A good end or good purpose does not justify any means. There might well be a worthy scientific goal which *ought not* be pursued if it unjustifiably violates another human good. In other words, ethical constraints might slow down, or even preclude, some scientific advances. The proliferation *of atomic armaments* is an obvious example; DNA research is possibly another.

The controversy surrounding recombinant DNA research should not be viewed solely from the perspective of a risk-benefit calculus. To frame the issues in terms of the increased knowledge and beneficial applications is to risk obscuring the other values at stake. There has been an urgency to recombinant DNA research which resulted in the formulation of guidelines in advance of research about the potential hazards of such research. That urgency should not be allowed to short circuit reflection on: the purpose and implications of these forms of DNA modification; the effect of this type of genetic research on the understanding of the human species and of its relation to nature; and the correlation between the scientific advance possible through recombinant DNA research and human progress as judged by a variety of criteria.

Discussion of the rights and limits of scientific inquiry in the instance of recombinant DNA well illustrates the necessity of striving always for open communication between science and the public. Such collaboration is necessary if wisdom and humility are to effect enlightened public policy.*

## When Human Life Begins?

The abortion question which has raged in the USA especially from 1973 onwards has revolved about scientific fact and analysis. The Supreme Court of the USA in its opinion said it could draw no time lines in the matter of human development, and then quite illogically divided the matter into numerically convenient tri-mesters, making very weak distinctions in each third, seemingly to sustain Chief Justice Burger's disclaimer that the decision did not sanction

---

*This section on DNA research is adapted from a 1977 statement of the National Conference of Catholic Bishops' Committee on Science, Technology and Human Values.

Bishop Hurley was chairman at the time; Sr. Ann Neale, as director, was chief author of the statement, which was edited and approved by the entire committee.

"abortion-on-demand." That position was immediately challenged in *Time* magazine, which called the decision "virtually" abortion-on-demand. The history of the question bears out *Time's* judgment.

Early on, the proponents designated the conceived being as just a piece of protoplasm; later, an organ of the mother. Some even appealed to St. Thomas Aquinas who opted, in his ignorance of biology, for a gradual hominization. Then came the woman's right, the pro-choice, and sadly, even sustaining the option to kill the unborn in the name of necessity, of convenience, and even of pure arbitrary choice. Next came the newest argument on just when life does begin with the Congressional hearings in May, 1981.

The hearings presented a curious metamorphosis in that some scientists were at pains to take the biological question out of the debate and appealed to theology and metaphysics, and hence, in their minds, to the realm of speculation and guess work. Theologians, on the other hand, were endeavoring to situate the matter precisely in the field of biology and life science as the primary datum upon which to build a coherent judgment of the facts.

Fr. Richard A. McCormick, S.J., of the Rose Kennedy Institute of Ethics in Washington, DC, one of the nation's leading authorities in the field of bioethics, summed up his answer, published in the *Washington Star* on March 23, 1981, in these words:

"Put a hundred reproductive biologists in a room together and ask them the question (when life begins). Their answer will be unanimous: at fertilization. The fertilized ovum is a living (not dead) human (not canine) being."

Similarly, Dr. Hymie Gordon of the Mayo Clinic's genetics department in Rochester, Minn., told a Congressional hearing (U.S. Senate, Judiciary Committee, April-June 1, 1981) that "...it is the first time I ever had to argue the unarguable...life begins at conception."

The Professor of Pediatrics and Obstetrics at the University of Pennsylvania, Dr. Alfred M. Bongiovanni, cited for the senators the standard textbooks on reproduction and concluded: "I received my medical education at the University of

Pennsylvania which is a non-sectarian private school. I have learned since my earliest medical education that human life begins at the time of conception."

He went on further to quote Dr. Gordon: " 'From the moment of fertilization when the deoxyribose nucleic acids from the spermatozoan and the ovum come together to form the zygote, the pattern of the individual's constitutional development is irrevocably determined...; true, environmental influences both during the intra-uterine period and after birth modify the individual's constitution and continue to do so right up to his death, but it is at the moment of conception that the individual's capacity to respond to these exogenous influences is established.

" 'Even at that early stage the complexity of the living cell is so great, it is beyond our comprehension.' " He concluded: "I submit that human life is present throughout this entire sequence from conception to adulthood and that any interruption at any point throughout this time constitutes the termination of human life."

Undaunted by the scientists who stated the case flatly and apodictically, Dr. Leon Rosenberg of Yale University department of genetics captured most of the media attention by insisting that actual human life (in utero, presumably) "is not a scientific (fact) but a religious, metaphysical one."

He pointedly repudiated the many scientists who had testified before him, dismissing them as men of personal prejudice: "If I am correct in asserting that the question of when actual life begins is not a scientific matter, then, you may ask, why have so many scientists come here to say that it is?

"My answer is that scientists, like all other people, have religious feelings to which they are entitled."

So often it has been the theologians and men of religion who have been accused of ignoring science, of contradicting the "facts" of biology, physics, astronomy, psychology, etc.; of imposing metaphysical concepts on science. Dr. Rosenberg and Supreme Court Justice Blackman, who wrote the Court's majority opinion, switched gears and pushed the question out of science and into speculation and hence gave themselves leeway for the conclusions they desired.

When asked by the Chairman, Senator East, when he would accept the fact of human life *in utero,* Dr. Rosenberg responded that as his "personal opinion...not speaking in the name of science...I would protect at the point of viability. I would protect at the point that the human being can exist on its own outside the uterus." He clearly would contradict the Supreme Court and State courts which have allowed the killing of the unborn right up to birth, far beyond viability—*pace,* the Edelin case in Massachusetts and the Waddell case in California.

Professor Jerome LeJeune, the famous geneticist and discoverer of the chromosomal defect which is the cause of the Down Syndrome (mongolism), member of the French academy, on April 23, 1981, testified directly to the issue, not only to the concept of the beginning of life, and the beginning of human life, but even to the notion of person:

"When does a person begin? I will try to give the most precise answer to that question actually available to science.

"Modern biology teaches us that ancestors are united to their progeny by a continuous material link.... Life has a very, very long history, but each individual has a very neat beginning: the moment of conception."

Citing the molecular thread of DNA as the link with ancestors, he added that "in each reproductive cell, this ribbon, roughly one meter long, is cut into pieces (23 in our species). Each segment is carefully coiled and packaged like a magnetic tape in a mini-cassette, so that under the microscope it appears like a little rod, a chromosome."

At the meeting of the male sperm and the female ovum, the father and mother each contribute 23 chromosomes to form a new human being "with the full genetic information." Somewhat like a symphony on a cassette "the new being begins to express himself as soon as he has been conceived."

LeJeune concluded that the whole genetic code necessary to build the body and especially the brain rests in a material substratum that could fit neatly on the point of a needle. "Even more impressive...each conceptus receives an entirely original combination (of genes) which has never occurred before and will never again. Each conception is unique and thus irreplaceable...: To accept the fact that, after fertilization has taken place, a new human being has come into being is no longer a matter of tests or of opinion. The human nature of the human being from conception to old age is not a metaphysical contention; it is plain experimental evidence.''

LeJeune concluded: "At two months of age, the human being is less than one thumb's length from head to the rump. He would fit in a nutshell but everything is there.... Science has turned the fairy-tale of Tom Thumb into a true story, the one each of us has lived in the womb of his mother.''

Any moral judgment must obviously begin with the facts, with reality, with what is involved. Science most often presents that data ahead of any moral or ethical judgment. Only when the facts, insofar as they can be understood, are presented can the judgment be made as to the rightness or wrongness of what is being proposed or actually being done. Atomic energy, radiation and its consequences, short-term and long-term effects, all are primary material for further judgment as to values and ethics. So with unborn life. The Church affirms the scientific fact that a new human life begins at fertilization.

There is, then, a very close and necessary relationship between scientists and moralists; between science and especially technology and religion, a relationship that demands both cooperation and collaboration. Scientists ignore human values; theologians ignore the discoveries of science to the peril of the human race. When human life begins is yet another case in point.

## The Test-Tube Baby

The birth in England on July 25, 1978, of the world's first test-tube baby—a baby conceived outside the womb and subsequently implanted in the womb of its mother—has attracted widespread attention. The baby, Louise Brown, is the daughter of Gilbert and Lesley Brown. An egg from the ovary of the mother, who could not conceive a baby naturally because her fallopian tubes were blocked, was used. No outside donor of sperm, i.e., other than her husband, was used.

The birth of the test-tube baby, as well as some other biomedical experiments, poses serious questions about marital and family life and could have profound implications for the future of society.

The news media have regularly reported stories telling of the artificial and manipulated conception of human life, some allegedly by "cloning"; others via the test-tube baby technique; still others through artificial insemination. These events in the sphere of science pose serious moral problems with both immediate and long-range consequences to which the Church and people of goodwill everywhere must respond with objectivity and in truth.

Scientists must be free to do their research which has been of such great blessing and benefit to mankind. Yet they cannot work in a vacuum, free from moral restraints, precisely because science does not generate its own values, much less determine human values.

Similarly, there must be sympathy and genuine compassion for spouses who desire children of their own. But in these cases, too, even where the immediate intentions are pro-child and pro-life, there are moral issues that cannot be evaded.

Society is facing not the mere possibility but the reasonable expectation that there can be a scientific fabrication of man and woman, the manipulation of human nature itself to construct a closed society according to some master plan with consequences dimly perceived but nonetheless quite real and foreboding. Other moral questions concern the methods of obtaining genetic components for these procedures; the destruction of "unacceptable" life samples; the control of the quality of life which subordinates the dignity and excellence of the human person to a social plan or a social destiny.

The moral consequences for family life and the unity of husband and wife in marriage are immediate. The Church teaches that "acts proper to married life are to be ordered according to authentic human dignity and must be honored with the greatest reverence" (Gaudium et Spes, no. 51). Science has succeeded, however, in giving men and women the means to separate in an artificial and even mechanical way sexual love and the begetting of new life.

On the one hand, sex has been blocked and frustrated in relation to the procreation of children, a condition that has made possible the contraceptive mentality so disastrous to society and nations. On the other hand, procreation has been separated from sexual love by these newest techniques. To the idea of "sex without babies," there is now added "babies without sex."

The Church, then, seeks moral judgments on these complex matters and precarious applications of technology. They cannot be solved simply by appealing to the good intentions of either scientists or doctors or the people involved. The Church teaches that in making these judgments, "God, the Lord of life, has entrusted to men the noble mission of safeguarding life, and men must carry it out in a manner worthy of themselves.... Objective criteria must be used, criteria drawn from the nature of the human person and human action, criteria which respect the total meaning of mutual self-giving and human procreation in the context of true love...."

Furthermore, it is to be noted that the couple desiring the baby were not themselves subjects of the experiment. A very high percentage of conceptions were deliberately aborted to obtain the "proper" one. The Protestant theologian and expert on bioethics, Paul Ramsey, has pointed out that there is a gratuitous presumption involved, namely, "that the mother has an absolute right to have a child." Leon Kass of the University of Chicago agrees in his article: "Babies by Means of In Vitro Fertilization: Unethical Experiments on the Unborn" (1971).

Testifying before the Ethics Advisory Board of the U.S. Department of Health, Education, and Welfare on December 4, 1978, Fr. Albert Moraczewski, O.P., opposed a federal policy that would underwrite test-tube babies. He based his opposition on "published scientific and medical data, on philosophical and theological reflection, and on the relevant teachings of the Church."

Himself a scientist, a pharmacologist who for eighteen years was on the staff at the Baylor Medical School in Texas, he exposed the interdisciplinary nature of any approach to the question of in vitro fertilization: science and medicine come first to establish the facts of the case; philosophy and theology look to value judgment, and the Church applies the gospel values, acceptable perhaps only to her own members.

He opposed in vitro fertilization on the grounds that it was not the treatment of a medical condition but of a desire; that no one has a strict right to another person, even to have a child; that the human embryo is exposed to unnecessary hazards without consent; even to the loss of life as well as genetic defects; that it violates the proper family environment for the generation of human beings, displacing a truly human act that is "the essential bonding act of the family"; that it is inimical to marriage.

Fr. Moraczewski cited Huxley's *Brave New World*, which portrayed a civilization in which children are generated solely in the laboratory from conception to birth, "all in glass, stainless steel, and shining chrome." The normal biological process is denounced as "animalistic."

The nature of marriage and the future of the family and society itself are at stake in these newest developments. With John Paul I, the Church welcomes life but not as an absolute.

## Prolonging Life and Euthanasia

The Church does not consider life an absolute, which means that life need not be preserved, protected, and nourished at all costs and without limitation: in a pagan ethic, direct killing of terminally ill patients is sanctioned. This practice is often designated as direct or active euthanasia. The opposite ethic that asks that every possible means to preserve life be employed is also unChristian for it exaggerates the importance of earthly existence.

All men, women, and children have a natural and normal obligation to take reasonable care of their health. At times even advanced equipment, technological devices, and "miracle" drugs might be considered not only as morally acceptable but even obligatory, e.g., where the father of a large young family might be saved.

Pope Pius XII in 1957 laid down some moral principles, the most fundamental being that though everyone has an obligation to use "ordinary" means to preserve his life, he is not obliged to use "extraordinary" ones. Thus such things as necessary food, rest, and shelter where possible would be essential at all times, no matter the case. Also the circumstances of person—whether a young father or a very elderly grandfather—of places and cultures (some sects proscribe blood transfusions), and even of time, should be taken into consideration.

With the rapid advances of science and technology, however, what was once "extraordinary" can become quite "ordinary" and even routine, such as intravenous feeding. Theologians have suggested a further refinement of this distinction: what is "reasonable" treatment and what "unreasonable" treatment. Obviously, reasonable treatment, given the circumstances of age, condition, obligations, even cost, chances of success, must be continued; unreasonable not.

The further moral question arises: who decides? especially for an unconscious patient?

The determination of prolonging life belongs primarily to the person himself or herself; in default, then to members of his family. Pope Pius XII stated that "The rights and duties of the family depend, in general, on the presumed will of the unconscious patient, if he is of age and *sui juris* (i.e., has attained the use of reason). As to the strict and independent duty of the family, it binds usually to the use of only ordinary means.

"Consequently, if it appears that the attempt at reanimation constitutes in reality such a burden for the family that one cannot in conscience force it on them, they can lawfully insist that the doctor cease his efforts, and the doctor can lawfully comply. In such a case there is no direct disposal of the life of the patient or euthanasia (mercy-killing), which would never be lawful."

The Pope also put the burden on the medical doctors as to the moment of death, calling it a "medical question" rather than one pertaining to religion or morals.

The Pope said that "it is for the doctors, and especially the anesthesiologist, to give a clear and precise definition of death and the moment of death." Philosophers and theologians would define death as the final separation of body and soul, but the concepts involved are too vague and too unspecific to answer the question of the moment of death based on philosophical ideas alone.

Heroic measures, therefore, are not of obligation for the sustenance of the human life of terminally ill and dying patients, whether in the womb or of advanced years. Neither are such measures required for seriously defective babies *in utero* or newly born. Sustaining human life, in other words, is a good to be sought, but it is not an absolute. Contrariwise, any judgment to omit treatment can never licitly be based upon the belief that certain human lives lack human worth and human dignity. The concept of "worthless life" applied to human beings is anti-Christian.

To omit life-saving therapy for an inadequate reason is evil. The mere omission of treatment may in itself be immoral; parents and family members, in consultation with physicians, for example, cannot just "let nature take its course" as a means of indirect killing of a patient.

The judgment in conscience will revolve about a cooperative assessment of the facts of the case between the family with men and women of science, and the family with men and women of religion, and the scientists with the theologians as to what is "reasonable" treatment and what "unreasonable."

## Patented Life

In its decision, on June 16, 1980, to allow the patenting of new forms of life created by scientists in their laboratories and test tubes, the Supreme Court of the USA in a 5 to 4 decision decided that current patent laws extend to living things.

Specifically, the Court has upheld the contention of the General Electric Company that it has the right to patent a bacterium modified through genetic engineering techniques. A researcher from India, Ananda Chakraharty, under the aegis of General Electric, developed bacteria which feed on oil, "eat it up" in a quick manner, thanks to special properties. These organisms can be protected by patent, the ruling went: "A live human-made micro-organism is patentable subject matter."

No one is immediately alarmed that these new microbe oil-eaters pose a great threat to humanity. But as man changes from creature to "creator" through laboratory fabrication of new life forms, he must link these discoveries with a right conscience or risk disaster.

Extreme reactions have greeted the decision: one group calling for the total ban of genetic experimentation; the other, mainly from the scientific and industrial communities, insisting that research should be unbridled and untrammeled.

To its credit, the Court envisioned deeper problems in the future, and invited Congress as the legislative branch of government to take a fresh look at patent laws in the light of these new phenomena. Down the road, the Court averred, much more serious questions of public policy will arise as "gene splicing" is developed and enhanced. The Church too must be in the vanguard of this new appraisal.

The Church should point out that banning all genetic research would deny too much good to the human race; but that uncontrolled experimentation could also result in great harm.

Pope John Paul II stated that applied science must be united with conscience because the human race has the possibility of becoming the victim of its own creation.

The field of genetic research portends many things for human life and human nature itself. It is theoretically possible that scientists could, in a sense, manufacture a "new" human being by combining the characteristics of one person with those of another or several more. Having broken the genetic code and mastered the manipulation of genes in lower life, scientists are moving inexorably to higher forms.

Genetic research and DNA techniques hold out much promise in the control and even cure of disease, in the production of food, and in the conservation of energy. Cancer and other diseases are now being attacked through the body's inner space, its genetic code. Gene transfers among plants seek to allow a food plant to receive a gene from another plant so that the food-producing plant can be enabled to take and to store nitrogen directly from the atmosphere, thus eliminating the heavy dependence on chemical fertilizers. Similarly, the production of insulin synthesized in a test tube through DNA research has reportedly already been achieved in the University of California laboratories and, subsequently, elsewhere. It is now being clinically tested and the results seem positive.

But there can be mistakes and accidents, too, and horrors fictionally explored in the movie "The Andromeda Strain." There can as well be a planned creation of disease-bearing microbes in a biological warfare waged to destroy human enemies as well as accidental results.

Should their "creators" enjoy the protection of patents over living creatures?

The theologian, Edwin L. Lisson, in *Hospital Progress*, January 1981, called for an appreciation of the relationships between the new technologies and patents on the one hand, and moral and ethical principles on the other.

"In the American system, at least in theory, the law subordinates the patent owner's rights and benefits to those of the common good....

"The critical response, then, is neither to condemn nor to bless categorically the technology of producing artificial life forms or patents granted for them."

The basic issues on the morality of patenting life forms concern the risks of diminishing human values by technology itself: to encourage the manufacture of patented forms of life without threatening basic human values. Does this technology presage the control of life, starting with the lower forms, for personal or corporate profit? Patents also promote monopolies, even if only for seventeen years.

On the other hand, patents can help to promote the dissemination of information which might otherwise be maintained as a trade secret.

There is yet another facet to the question not addressed by the Court. Most of the research in the field of genetics and DNA related to new biological organisms, to agriculture, and to energy is being financed by the government, to wit, the taxpayers of the USA.

Should not this work and its results be readily available to the general public, such as the polio vaccine was? Should researchers, many of whom have already formed private corporations, or signed up with giant private companies, become instant millionaires, protected by patent, and further subsidized by the same taxpayers who will have to pay much more because of these same patents?

The tentative language of the Supreme Court calls for Congress and the public to take an objective look at this whole new era of technology and research with its beneficent promises and portentous dangers. Private enterprise has a legitimate role, and so does the Church. Patents over inventions are one thing; patents over micro-organisms are quite another.

The genetic revolution, with its problems and achievements so close to the general public, so close to the human species, so close to human nature itself, presents a stupendous challenge to all mankind to resolve the "new values" it is generating.

# CHAPTER FIVE

## COMPUTERS, DATA BANKS, AND HUMAN FREEDOM

> "In our day, advances in science and technology have greatly multiplied relationships between citizens...(which must) be brought into more humane balance."
> John XXIII, *Pacem in Terris*, no. 212

Science and technology have scarcely been more successful in cooperating to establish a new and almost radically different application of genius to modern society, whether in government, commerce and industry, medicine, scholarship, and even art, than in what is properly called the "computer revolution" or the "electronic revolution." The ramifications of this revolution and its impact on human life and liberty are staggering, and only dimly perceived.

Potential for the establishment of the all-powerful government, for the totalitarian state; for the reduction of persons to numbers in an all-encompassing central system under central control; for the invasion of privacy, both individual, familial, and corporate, cannot be thought to be yet in the realm of science fiction. Marshall McLuhan, in his famous dictum that the medium is the message, identified the electronic "eyes" of photos from space, photos through walls, sonar and radar, and surveillance devices, "eyes" which pierced almost all security. He identified the electronic "ear," which snooped on people's personal lives with wiretaps and listening devices. More importantly, he recognized the "electronic memory" which recorded the sights and sounds and made them permanent, a matter of record not in stone but potentially more lasting and quickly retrievable. There has been born of computers and data banks—even more ominously than bugging devices, wiretaps, and secret cameras and radar thrusts— a serious threat to the privacy, intimacy, seclusion, and personal dignity in society at all levels of human sociability and social relationships.

Some states in the USA moved to protect privacy through legislation, even by constitutional amendment as science in its inevitable and inexorable progress put new and potentially more dangerous tools into the hands of mankind.

The electronic revolution, even as the genetic revolution, calls for moral and ethical judgment. When science meets the human, or better, when applied science or technology touches the human race, value judgments must be made—judgments that call for "right" and "wrong."

The citizens of California awoke on the morning of November 8, 1972, to read in the daily papers that they had amended their State Constitution by the passage of Proposition XI. Proposition XI? What in heaven was that?

There had been practically no campaign of any appreciable magnitude *pro* or *con*. The press, surprisingly, by-and-large did not show enthusiastic support or intense opposition, but generally took the view that the proposition was unnecessary, redundant, already a matter of law. Opponents labeled it a scheme to protect welfare fraud on the part of the poor and tax evasion on the part of the rich. Even the guardians of the law, judges and lawyers, took little or no notice. Proposition XI by all odds was a "sleeper," and the people passed it by a large majority. It involved only three words: "people" and "and privacy."

The first article of the State Constitution now reads: "Inalienable Rights: All *people* are by nature free and independent and have certain inalienable rights, among which are those enjoying and defending life and liberty; acquiring, possessing, and protecting property; and pursuing and obtaining safety, happiness, *and privacy.*"

The substitution of the word "people" for "men" may well be claimed as a victory for women's liberation; the addition of "privacy" to the inalienable rights an earnest and a harbinger of things to come, involving the executive, legislative, judicial branches of government, not to mention the political, philosophical, and theological implications.

With the astonishing growth and amazing development of technology—and specifically the computer, magnetic tapes, and microfilms—there has been born concomitantly an insatiable appetite for information-gathering by government and by private enterprise, a gourmand hunger and endless craving to gather, store, and retrieve data of all kinds. Moreover, "throughout the public and private sectors, the amount of information collected and stored about individuals is increasing at exponential rates." This appetite for information is at once desultory, capricious, and dangerous.

Thanks to the Watergate "caper," the Pentagon papers trial, and similar escapades, electronic surveillance has captured the attention of the nation. Reports of army intelligence agents spying on civilians during civilian riots and protest marches; the "prophecies" to foretell potential rioters; the bugging of offices, public and private; wiretaps and videotapes and all the rest make chilling reading.

But even more ominous and portentous is the potential inherent in the technology which has given birth to data banks and methods of systems analysis which technology encourages. With speed akin to light, gifted with a prodigious memory, data banks are becoming the repository of a vast amount of information about people—data that can be kept in storage indefinitely.

The Constitutional Rights Subcommittee of the Senate sponsored a study (1969) which noted, *inter alia,* that the more economical computer technology has become, the more "an army of specialists in the information-processing field...and battalions of investigators and analysts specializing in seeking out and reporting derogatory information on individuals" grow and wax strong. Zeal to know the "total man" has kept government and private computers filling dossiers "to overflowing with the daily lives of people."

Computers have come of age, and data banks have achieved a sophistication suggestive of Orwell's *1984.*

The Federal Government has at least twenty-seven agencies and bureaus gathering information, much of it quite private and personal. The Department of Health, Education, and Welfare, and now its successor department, the Department of Health and Human Services, "owns" the social security numbers. It used to be that a youth would receive his social security number when he got his first job. Today that number may be assigned upon entrance into first grade or even before. Can the newborn babe escape? The answer is "no." The Internal Revenue Service, now computerized, gathers tax return data; similarly, the Passport Bureau; welfare departments; civilian personnel departments in government; the Department of Commerce with its file on seafarers; the Census Bureau; the Center for Health Statistics; the Department of Justice; the Bureau of Narcotics; the Naturalization Service; the Department of State with its "lookout file"; the Customs Bureau; the Secret Service; the F.B.I.; the C.I.A., etc., all seek data, much of it private and personal, not to mention confidential and compromising in some instances.

Employers in the private sector are wont to gather personal information of prospective employees, seeking even security clearances, at times without the subjects themselves having any access to these same records. In an economy heavily dependent on credit, bankers make extensive use of computers; credit-card companies build credit dossiers on millions of customers. A fairly accurate profile of a person's actions can be constructed from the transactions of a steady credit-card user. Doctors, too, build up files—often of a very personal and intimate nature. Seven hundred life insurance companies rely upon the Medical Information Bureau of Boston to check prospective insurees. Student records are a major source of information for dozens of purposes, from the granting of scholarships to employment. Even the driver's license has become a source of special attention; many states have sold drivers' lists commercially.

Finally, not merely the criminal records of all law enforcement agencies, but their general files as well—the police files—contain vast quantities of information, much of it confidential and, at times, compromising to individuals and groups.

The potential for dossier-building staggers the imagination; the womb-to-tomb history of each person retrievable on demand becomes a possibility, at the very least.

But what if all these files and dossiers could be centralized, cross-referenced, and, in one place, made available? Is it possible to evolve the "total identifier" in a master-file, perhaps under the social security number?

Pressures to introduce a single identifying number for each citizen, known as S.I.N., have come from both private and public sources. The advantages of S.I.N. are obvious for hospitals, credit card companies, schools, banks, police, and others. All chartered banks in the USA, for example, have been required to record the social security numbers of depositors to facilitate the retrieval of information for tax purposes, a breach in the initial law on social security. Contrariwise, Congress refused to allow the social security number cross-reference on the 1970 census forms.

Sweden introduced identification numbers for all citizens in 1947; Israel in 1948, Norway, 1964: and other countries expected to follow suit include Benelux countries, West Germany, Spain, Japan and Switzerland.

The single identification number and the concomitant "total identifier" pose both a temptation and a threat. The enormous value in time saved, in costs, in accuracy, whether to employers, police, the I.R.S., banks, life insurance companies, doctors, and educators, can scarcely be exaggerated and constitute a real temptation. At the same time, in terms of individual—and even corporate and institutional—liberties, they pose a threat of no mean proportions. A master-file under a single social security number does not now exist; the U.S. Health, Education and Welfare Department (HEW) study of this matter states, however, that "automated personal data systems present a serious potential for harmful consequences, including infringement of basic liberties."

In his *Data Banks in a Free Society*, Alan F. Westin labels as "mostly fantasy" the image of computers storing up data, talking among themselves, and linking up tapes and discs to form a surveillance net from which no fact about an individual's life can escape. Vast *centralized* computer data banks simply do not exist, despite a widespread conviction to the contrary in the mass media and the public.

Experts affirm that it is scarcely feasible economically to store data of vast magnitude *directly* in the "on line" memory of the computer. But they also point out that the computer can be programmed to key in on the "off-line" memory with data stored on discs, magnetic tapes, and on microfilm, as well as cards. The Taxation Division of Canada, for example, stores on 125 reels of magnetic tape the records of 10½ million taxpayers, consisting of 500 characters each. At the same time, all experts agree that computers will become smaller in size, more versatile in operation, and much less expensive to purchase and operate.

While the "total identifier" does not as yet exist, it cannot so easily be dismissed as not feasible simply on economic grounds. Rather, Westin's study recommends a social and legal policy be effected "with built-in safeguards hammered out before the inevitable development of *centralized* computer record-keeping."

A Canadian Government task force in its study, *Privacy and Computers* (1972), which enjoyed "close liaison" with Professor Westin's study group, stated in its opening words the dimensions of its work: "The widespread development of highly computerized data banks has given rise to increasing concern about their potential use for invasions of personal privacy." This study rejected the proposition that invasions of privacy are so widespread as to cause alarm. Yet "continuing worries exist" because "few data banks have been designed and installed with a concern for privacy built into the planning process, except for institutional self-interest."

"The privacy crisis," the study concludes, "unlike the ecology crisis, which was predicted but largely ignored until severe damage had been done to the environment, *need never happen.* Appropriate preventive measures can make certain it never will."

While there is no doomsday syndrome forming in this matter, no need for prophets of doom, yet the Canadian task force warns that "insensitive or willful use of the computer could lead us closer to *1984.*"

The city of Huntington Beach, California, is reported in the press to be the first American community to have entered each one of its citizens—man, woman, child, guilty or innocent, accused or unindicted—on its police department's computer. On the basis of home address, the data includes medical information, abandoned cars, water bills, credit history, and even the name of the family dog. Financial support came from the Law Enforcement Assistance Administration of the Federal Government. The question can reasonably be asked if the citizens of Huntington Beach or anywhere else in the USA realize the extent and range of information-gathering going on without their knowledge in many, if not most, cases. Do they realize that dossiers are being built up without the possibility of review and correction of "raw files" and "raw data"; without the knowledge of who—in or out of government—has access to these files?

The same Law Enforcement Assistance Administration has pumped millions of dollars into state and local police departments to promote computerization, "108 computer projects in 1971" alone. Similarly the FBI-managed National Crime Information Center is creating a network which ultimately will join over 6,000 law-enforcing agencies, a single source of data.

"All of these trends must be looked at as a unit because their confluence represents a terrifying specter," writes law professor Authur Miller.

One need only reflect on the Watergate hearings to note that "informal" interchanges of FBI files took place between the Attorney General's office and the Committee to Re-elect the President. The computer hasn't much changed the methods of political campaigns, but it has made such exchanges easier, more efficient, and most tempting. Moreover, under the old manual files, it was possible to get away from one's past and begin again a new life free of damaging information.

The modern political campaign is now committed to computers and data banks as essential tools; not only successful candidates, but defeated ones as well keep their voter lists, now easily processed, for future reference. The sale of such lists has become big business.

Technology, however, promises to create a "dossier prison" wherein every entry will remain for life, a possible "hearsay narrative" without literal or contextual accuracy. The prospective employee may be asked if he were ever "arrested." Even though subsequently acquitted, his "yes" answer may well foredoom his chance for employment. The computer will keep that "fact" indefinitely. In his official inquiry for the House of Representatives, Congressman Cornelius Gallagher contrasted the Judeo-Christian concept "to forgive and forget, to make amends and begin again" with the "computer that cannot forget and that is incapable of forgiving."

Assemblyman Kenneth Cory, who introduced the "privacy" amendment in California, summed up the matter in these words: "The frightening thing about many of these files is the individual may never know he is in them or who has seen the information recorded.... If this information were centralized and augmented (by cross-reference files), government could truly know more about many of us than we know ourselves."

The June 25, 1973, *U.S. News and World Report* published, "A Fight Over Who Can Look at Your Tax Return" which reported that a presidential order to open the income-tax returns of 3 million farmers to the U.S. Department of Agriculture had engendered a reaction in Congress described as "explosive." The Department sought the requested data "on tapes" directly from the IRS computers at Martinsburg, W.VA.

In 1981, the courts sought to protect the IRS from a taxpayer, who wanted to know what formulas are used to determine whose returns are audited. The computers are now programmed to catch the "cheaters"; the formula remains secret.

Senator Sam Ervin, of Watergate fame, has recited a litany of offenses against personal privacy: the selling or lending of lists of names on government files; the sharing of "black lists" among agencies; the sharing of credit lists; check on the finances, sex life, personal beliefs, and associations of famous and unknown people alike; and even the questioning of women by the Federal Housing Administration on birth control practices, the private advice of doctors, in reference to loans on homes. "Unchecked, we will have the trappings of a police state," he concluded.

One technical expert said simply: "Considering what I know about micro-electronics, I must conclude that the worst is yet to come. We must manage the keepers of the machines!"

## The Physical Climate

Computer technology and data banks serve men and are controlled by humans. They are not autonomous. But who controls the human factor? Who protects not only the individual citizen, but as well groups, associations, corporate entities, racial and ethnic and religious assemblies from the mis-use and abuse of technological data gathering? How control the insatiable appetite and inordinate zeal of some of those in power, whether in the public or private sector? *Quis custodit custodem?* Who will watch the watcher?

The computer is a many-splendored animal; consequently, there is much potential protection right in the technology itself, sophisticated means whereby safeguards can be part and parcel of the data banks themselves. Most observers call for new laws. Others, while conceding the role of law, would add the need for a public morality and moral consensus on the protection of privacy. But no data bank system can ever be fully secure, and "security measures can be broken if the pay-off warrants the trouble." Thus, physical security and control of access as well as steps taken to insure honest personnel are at least as important as some of the sophisticated protection measures programmed in the computer system itself.

Computer systems use such devices as "passwords" stored in two places, i.e., with the user and the system, for the retrieval of data; various codes for scrambling and unscrambling data; limited access control not only as to "who" but as to access to "what"; audit trails to detect unauthorized usage. IBM, for example, has announced an investment of $40 million in the next few years to develop security protective hardware for its computer systems.

With its wondrous capacity to accept, store, and retrieve information, the computer in its very sophistication can as easily be programmed to destroy data. Medical facts, for example, can be processed for research and statistical purposes and then "forgotten." Similarly the facts may be stored but the identity of the human subject erased. Furthermore, the computers can be "taught" to require the identity of the person who takes information.

The salient point is, however, that security up to this date has been geared towards the protection of industrial and political security against espionage, and *not* in the context of individual privacy. Data banks that contain sensitive information require technical programming that protects the human right to privacy insofar as is reasonable. Much can be done, then, to build in certain safeguards. But such is but a first step; the law of the land must reckon the new technology and its ramifications even beyond the invasion of privacy.

## The Legal Climate

This legal approach to the protection of privacy is not so simple. To leave it to the courts and judiciary will not solve the problem of proper protection; nor will legislatures solve the questions alone. There is a necessary interplay between the judiciary and legislative branches of government; but equally there is similar relationship between them and the administrative and regulatory agencies of government.

Courts can be slow; litigation, costly and time-consuming. Principles are developed over a long period, case-by-case; the redress of wrongs is *past* history. More is needed, yet the court's role is crucial.

Similarly, the need for new laws will undoubtedly emerge, as challenges, particularly to the regulatory agencies, are raised. Yet the key question seems to be: Is there a superior public interest to which individuals must yield their privacy?

"The right to know," or "freedom of information" must be measured against "the right to be left alone" and "the fact that it is none of the government's business." A private individual (and association) has a basic and continuing interest in not having information about himself communicated to other people without his knowledge, or contrary to his will. Such information may be detrimental, or may cause him pain or discomfort. Particularly are the poor and the weak vulnerable, for often they cannot sustain such revelation emotionally or even economically. Unwanted and unwarranted publicity often inflicts unnecessary psychological and subtle pressures. Where then do the contending social values override this private interest?

The U.S. Constitution in its Bill of Rights rejects specific invasions of privacy in the matters of religion, speech, unreasonable search and seizure, self-incrimination. The 4th and 5th Amendments in particular delineate a sphere of privacy which must be protected against governmental intrusion. Further, the Court has repudiated the mode of action by government whereby investigative authority abridges the right to privacy in order to determine if the right itself should be abridged in the public interest. Similarly, the right to privacy extends to groups and associations.

"It is beyond debate that freedom to engage in association for the advancement of beliefs and ideas is an inseparable aspect of 'liberty' assured by the...14th Amendment" (Harlan, 357 US460). The inviolability of privacy in group association may well be essential to the preservation of freedom of association itself.

But has not the new technology with its computerized data banks opened up new loopholes, potencies, and challenges to both courts and legislatures?

The U.S. Supreme Court (Couch vs. U.S.), on January 9, 1973, wrestled with the problem of privacy. While it did not deal with the new technology, it did perhaps lay foundations for future decisions.

By court action a tax accountant was required to produce a client's records, books, bank statements, cancelled checks, etc., "and all other pertinent documents pertaining to tax liability of the above taxpayer." The defendant claimed the right to privacy; the court denied the plea, disallowing as "privileged" the relationship between tax accountant and client, nor "as an invasion of privacy" the government regulatory agency's demand to see files once turned over to the accountant. The court decided that *in this case* the claim to immunity and privacy leaps the proper bounds and interferes with the legitimate interests of society in the enforcement of its laws and the collection of revenues. Yet the court spoke language that would indicate its concern for personal privacy.

"By its very nature," the Court wrote, "the privilege (against self-incrimination) is an intimate and personal one. It respects a private inner sanctum of individual feeling and thought, and proscribes state-intrusion to extract self-condemnation...(affirming) the right of each individual 'to a private enclave where he may lead a private life'...."

California court decisions are probably somewhat typical of other states' judicial decisions. The right of privacy is recognized under existing California law and has been defined in a general sense as living one's life in seclusion without being subjected to unwarranted and undesired publicity.

The Office of Legislative Counsel of California (July 7, 1972) summarized the matter in these words:

"1. The right of privacy was unknown to ancient common law.

"2. It is an incident of the person and not of property....

"3. It is a purely personal action and does not survive but dies with the person.

"4. It does not exist where the person has published the matter complained of or consented thereunto.

"5. It does not exist where a person has become so prominent that by his very presence he has dedicated his life to the public and thereby waives his right to privacy. There exists no right of privacy for that which is already public.

"6. It does not exist in the dissemination of news and news events, nor in the discussion of events of the life of a person in whom the public has a rightful interest nor where the revelation would be of public benefit, as in the case of a candidate for public office.

"7. The right of privacy can only be violated by printings, writings, pictures or other permanent publications or reproductions, and not by word of mouth...."

Further, the courts have raised the question as to who controls the circulation of personal information, and who has access to legitimate records.

While the courts have long been active in the area of "privacy," and even the U.S. Supreme Court based its decision in the Connecticut contraception case (Griswold) on the right to privacy, the legal experts, judging from the law school reviews, labeled the decision as "none-too-clear" yet "the clearest to date" on the "elusive nature of privacy," "a broad, abstract, ambiguous concept."

Nor have the legislatures fared much better. Their work on the protection of privacy has been judged "spotty and non-comprehensive." The administrative branches of government have patently failed in serious ways as the recitations of the invasions of privacy grow longer and sadder, to wit, the record of wiretaps, electronic surveillance right in the President's own offices; the sterilization of young girls with or without parental consent under the aegis of governmental agencies and at taxpayers' expense; the experimentation on human beings with venereal disease, etc., etc.

Patently there are new dimensions to the problems of privacy in society today, problems exacerbated by technology itself.

Health and Human Services (HHS), the regulatory agency in the Federal Government most deeply concerned with the information gathered on individuals, has been working on a study towards the protection of the right of privacy. As "owner" of the social security numbers (and who does not now have a social security number?), HHS is particularly the target of information seekers, computer-experts, and all those devoted to S.I.N., the single identifying number.

The agency, at the request of the President of the United States, has drafted proposals for safeguarding personal information. Its faith in its project may be summed up in its draft report: "The application of automated data processing technology to the management of records containing personal data can be subjected to appropriate and effective social constraint without diminishing its usefulness.

"We share strongly the belief," it goes on to say, "that protective action should be taken and that the Department (HEW) has a unique opportunity and responsibility to help safeguard against and overcome the potentially harmful consequences of automated personal data systems."

To such ends the Committee has proposed rules and regulations by way of safeguards to privacy.

One person should be responsible for the proper security and safeguards. Data must be eliminated after it is no longer truly useful, a sort of statute of limitations. Public notices must be posted when, for example, an agency has an automated personal data system. The agency must not only say it has such a system, but the categories of persons on whom data is kept as well; kinds, sources, and uses of data kept. Who has access to data, how individuals may get redress, and what is legally required must be made a matter of public record.

But while HHS struggles with the problems, what of the private sector? Who has more sensitive and all-embracing information of a personal nature *in one place* than the central data bank in Boston, the resource center for 700 insurance companies? What of the huge credit card operations of Master Charge, Visa, Bank of America, and American Express? Such questions have prompted Professor Miller to call upon "credit agencies and insurance companies (to) achieve a minimal level of *ethical* activity in the gathering of information."

Miller has advocated, in answer to the total problem, the formation of "an independent, non-operating agency specifically concerned with the task of monitoring information systems and preventing abuse," a National Data Center as first proposed by Richard Ruggles.

## The Moral Climate

But when all is said and done, there still remains the moral climate in which the judicial, legislative, and administrative branches of government, as well as private enterprise, live and breathe and have their being. A moral climate is fundamental to the solving of the problem of the threatened invasion of privacy. If Watergate has said anything, it has called for an ethical refurbishing of the climate of our society.

Theologians raised in the "natural law" tradition see the right of privacy, like the right to think, as deriving from the human personality "with no direct connection with the mission of the state." The natural law and the *jus gentium* demand privacy; people must be secure in consulting professional people in their personal problems; in the use of the mails; in the sanctuary of their homes.

Much like its legal history, the concept of "privacy" in moral theology in the Church has not been met head-on. Treatment of privacy centers mostly in the subject of "secrecy." Secrets must be kept inviolate to avoid pain, offense, loss to the "owner" of a secret. Such a right is, of course, not absolute, except in the sacrament of confession. Secrets must be kept in order to insure free and confident access to the various levels of professional advice, and a violation of such secrets is an offense against social justice. A breach of secrecy demands a delicate assessment of all relevant factors, such as serious injury to an innocent third party, or national security, etc.

On a related matter of the "invasion" of the human mind and possible invasion of privacy, Pope Pius XII in 1958 warned psychoanalysts that "just as it is illicit to appropriate another's goods, to make an attempt on his bodily integrity without his consent, so it is not permissible to enter his inner domain against his will."

Thus there is a natural secrecy from the nature of the human person and of society itself protecting individuals and groups from harm or reasonable displeasure.

It can be fairly concluded that while the bases for the protection of privacy do exist in law and moral theology, yet the right to privacy has not been sufficiently enunciated in either, particularly in view of the advent of modern tools of information gathering and the temptations thereunto attached.

Some experts are calling for "a total and complete revamping of our legislative approach to informational privacy, including the regulation of computer transmissions and the movement of information in interstate commerce" (Miller). Most will admit that an "ethical refurbishing" is necessary, a change in the moral climate in the USA to protect the individual and groups against the threatened invasion of privacy, a value among those few values so fundamental and yet so undefined.

As was well stated in Stanley vs. Georgia (394 US, 564), the right to privacy is an aspect of the spiritual nature of man: "The makers of our Constitution undertook to secure conditions favorable to the pursuit of happiness. They recognized the significance of man's spiritual nature, of his feelings, and of his intellect. They knew that only a part of the pain, pleasure and satisfactions of life are to be found in material things. They sought to protect Americans in their beliefs, their thoughts, their emotions, and their sensations. They conferred, as against the government, the right to be let alone—the most comprehensive of rights and the right most valued by civilized man."

That "many-splendored animal," the computer, promises great benefits and poses equally serious threats. New safeguards are in order and are imperative.

The people of California were walking much in advance of their legislators, judges, administrators, and theologians when they voted affirmatively that the right to privacy should be singled out, underscored, and emphasized in this our day and times. Implicitly, they agreed with the judgment that "The privacy crisis, unlike the ecology crisis which was predicted but largely ignored until severe damage had been done to the environment, need never happen!"

Science is being asked to build in its own controls: the law is being challenged to vindicate rights in the overwhelming rush for data now available through technology; and the Church is being asked to update its moral theology, in light of the electronic age, to foster a moral climate respecting the dignity of the human person, including freedom from the fear of having his private life cataloged indefinitely for the unjust scrutiny of others, whether individuals, corporations, or the state.

# CHAPTER SIX

## THE SCIENTIFIC AND THE SECULAR IN THE USA

> "When...developed countries assist
> the poorer ones, they not only should
> have regard for (their own individual
> characteristics...and cultural tradi-
> tions), but also take special care,
> lest in aiding these nations, they
> seek to impose their own way of life
> upon them.... This clearly would be
> only another form of colonialism."
> John XXIII, *Mater et Magistra,*
> no. 169ff.

The United States has been undergoing a process of "secularization," wherein the autonomy of science has been more and more accepted; wherein the Church and Churches have been accorded less and less influence in education; and wherein there has been a drift into "secularism" which is at root a radical denial of God's place in the world. At best God has been considered irrelevant to life and learning; at worst His very existence is denied.

Papal teaching has made a distinction between "secularization" and "secularism." The former accepts the legitimate autonomy not only of governments and institutions but as well of intellectual disciplines, sciences, and even technology. There is in this concept no exclusion of God nor of the Church nor of morality, but rather a mutual respect for the province and competence of each.

"Secularism," on the other hand, relegates God, religion, and the Church to a totally private sphere; it, in effect, denies the existence of God and any relationship of the human race to any transcendent being.

There is also a sense in which secularism denies primarily the Providence of God (explaining by human prevision) which denial leads to an ignoring of God and all that such a belief in the Judeo-Christian, Moslem and other religious traditions imply not only for morality but for civilization itself. A logical distinction may be made between the denial of the existence of God and the denial of His Providence or interest in the human race. In practice, the denial of Providence often leads to the denial of the existence of God.

Speaking in broad terms, the USA is neither atheistic nor agnostic. It is rather "man-centered," passionately subjective, and the questions of God, human destiny and salvation simply do not arise. Many Americans are radically concerned with freedom almost to the absolute degree: freedom from God and His law, from any law, and even from the "tyranny of creation." Many worship, not the God of revelation, or even of theodicy, but *man* and machines he creates and engineers. His certitude comes vaguely from what he loosely calls "science." Human values enjoy an autonomy free from the influence of religion, which is relegated to a purely private sphere; free from any transcendent moral principles.

In search of a prophet or philosopher of "science," the intellectual easily chooses the father of positivism, Auguste Comte, who described society and *all* disciplines as moving inexorably through three stages in rigid succession: the theological or fictitious, the metaphysical or abstract, and finally, the highest stage, the positive or "scientific." He judged in 1830 that natural science had already transcended and succeeded both the religious and metaphysical in favor of the "scientific": he accordingly propounded as a conclusion the "religion of humanity." His theories found a warm reception in England through John S. Mill, and were popularized in the USA by John Dewey, prophet par excellence of empiricism and pragmatism.

## The Dehumanization of Man

The obvious and enormous benefits to man coming from the progress of science and technology, benefits on a practical level such as the lightening of physical work, the avoidance of pain, the prevention and cure of disease, instant and world-wide communications, swift transportation, and electronic tools have tempted modern man to judge, as a logical conclusion, that the question of the very existence of God or of the destiny of man beyond the grave is unnecessary and indeed quite irrelevant. Such a conclusion, needless to add, constitutes a serious threat to man, to society, and to civilization itself.

The process of the dehumanization of man continues apace, and is to be found precisely, and, in its potential, in the progress of science and technology when directed by a secularist ideology. Man has new knowledge and new tools to apply to science and civilization. The results stagger the imagination, actually, and in future promise, by the same token, they auger great mischief. By the denial of man's true nature, the secularizers, positivists, and humanists pose a serious and imminent threat to man's freedom. That the dehumanization of man may be the result of unbridled and laissez-faire capitalism as well as Marxism-Leninism is conceded. Perhaps even a more pervasive and universal threat has its origin and dynamic in modern science and technology.

## The Secular Not a Scapegoat

One must avoid the temptation to make a "scapegoat" out of the "secular."

The increased autonomy of the secular does not spell the end of religion or of religious concerns; while the religious dimension still holds the 20th century man's interest, yet he is restive and alienated in his new world. He finds himself submerged, in the USA and elsewhere in the world, in material abundance and technical achievement, a prodigious consumer of goods and services, at times to the detriment of the true depth of his being and the quality of his life. While he admires "science," he sees no scientific utopia as promised, and hence lives in doubt and uncertainty. Many people, not the least the youth of the decades of the 60's and 70's, are asking the religious question: the nature of God and man; the meaning of life and death. Even those who seem not to have even an obscure consciousness of the existence of God, nonetheless are convinced, in the light of the history of the 20th century, undoubtedly the most bloody century on record, that science of itself cannot bring happiness.

The Church, too, must answer for its use of God's creation, its relation to the "secular," to science and technology which uncover the secrets latent in the works of the Creator. The Catholic Church must ask the right questions about "secular" society, at once so promising and so ominously threatened; it must use its prophetic voice to sustain science and to bring the Gospel principles on its application to the human race. In science and technology among the family of nations, the United States stands pre-eminent even though its pre-eminence is now seriously challenged.

## The USA in Scientific Research and Technology

Few advances in science in the future will be made in splendid isolation; the day of the genius-scientist working alone in a laboratory seems over. New discoveries rather will be the results of teamwork in very elaborate and sophisticated circumstances. The use of exotic energy such as nuclear power; of complex electronic computer systems; and consummate cooperation among scientists in their special fields of competence costs amounts of money possible only to governments such as that of the USA and the wealthiest private foundations and universities. Moreover, the total dedication and full-time energy demanded of some scientists not only calls for huge expenditures, but precludes the distractions of even the classic academic environment of universities in favor of research teams living and working together in isolated retreats known as "think tanks."

For some years, too, the USA has been luring scientists from other countries in what has been aptly described as a "brain drain" in support of research. The literature of science, once a stream emanating from Europe, especially from Germany and Great Britain to the New World, now has been reversed sharply. That the USA first put man on the moon is neither an accident nor surprising when one considers the all but astronomical cost in time, talent and treasure.

The pre-eminent position of the USA in science and technology challenges the future of science itself. In that future there looms serious challenges to society, to the dignity of man, and to the Church itself.

The pre-eminent position of scientists in the society in which they live puts in their hands a power and potential out of proportion to their competency in their own fields of research. It becomes a very easy step for the general public, dazzled by the undoubted excellence of research and the manifest benefits to society, to grant the same authority to scientists even when they speak and act *outside* their respective competencies. By a curious transfer of training, scientists properly honored by Nobel prizes for scientific research often became oracles in fields foreign to their work, especially in matters of religion, morality, and justice. Linus Pauling and James Watson come easily to mind; the one for the application of quantum physics to chemistry; the other for his work in the discovery of the structure of DNA.

The result has become a form of neo-religion in the USA, a religion of humanity, in which scientific discoveries and technology constitute their own morality and ethical norms for the human race. Shades of Comte in academic circles, and Dewey in the marketplace.

## The USA as Exporter of Morals

Thanks to its leadership in science and technology, the USA has been able to export a steady flow of scientific information and sophisticated technology to the rest of the world, much, if not most of it to the great benefit of men and nations.

Yet simultaneously the USA, often in deliberate conscious manner, has sent as well its secular ethic along with its valuable assistance. There is the rising suspicion that the acceptance of this secular ethic has not been too subtly posited as a condition or sine-qua-non for such assistance. The USA has exported a secular ethic and moral judgments contrary to the Judeo-Christian heritage and culture, and even contrary to the basic American rationale as expressed in the Declaration of Independence of 1776. It is a neo-colonialism based on power, the power of money and science.

## Moral Imperialism

The USA has at times succumbed to the temptation to "moral imperialism." It sees US tax money being poured into foreign countries in the form of aid conditioned by the acceptance of abortion, artificial birth-control, sterilization and other eugenic measures. The transistor radios exported to the Third World as "rewards" for vasectomies for male sterilization are well known. In his book *Governing America: An Insider's Report from the White House and Cabinet,* 1981, Joseph Califano, Secretary of HEW, reports that "President Johnson was an ardent proponent of birth control at home and abroad. He repeatedly rejected the unanimous pleas of his advisors from Secretary of State Dean Rusk to National Security Advisor Walt Rostow to ship wheat to starving Indians during their 1966 famine. He demanded that the Indian government first agree to mount a massive birth control program. The Indians finally moved and Johnson released the wheat over a sufficiently extended period to make certain the birth control program was off the ground.

"Johnson spoke so often and forcefully about birth control that the Catholic bishops denounced him publicly."

There was a similar treatment within its own borders of the poor, the displaced, the aged, the prisoner, wherein tax money was used to support an ethic and morality at fundamental variance with the historic US culture and tradition, not to mention the natural moral law. Several examples have been cited above in Chapter Three.

Over the years the National Conference of Catholic Bishops has challenged the government, private foundations, scientific and technological associations, the legal and medical professions and others in the USA and will continue to challenge this "moral imperialism" both within and outside the boundaries of the country. A knowledge of this fact alone may suggest to those in other countries, especially the clergy and laity, a similar resistance to this exportation of morals concomitant with forms of assistance and aid, from basic food to exotic electronic equipment, from basic medicine to public health services.

Much attention has been given to "political" strings attached to foreign aid by the larger, more affluent nations. Overt or covert coercion in matters of personal morals, or in social moral patterns, corrupts the very generosity which prompted assistance in the first place.

The great sacrifices, the altruistic virtues, and the genius of the people of USA in support of less favored nations and peoples are a blessing. The uncritical and undifferentiated, simplistic attacks on the USA and its generous people in the name of "anti-capitalism" is wide of the mark. Yet the Church has not hesitated to point out, in a spirit of candor and objectivity, the serious problems attendant on foreign-aid programs which, under the mantle of the benefits of science and technology, export an insidious morality to other nations which threatens to de-humanize man and society.

By reason of the pre-eminence of the USA in science and technology, and its role as a leader in the political and economic sphere, the Church has sought to study science from a moral viewpoint, to understand man in a society in the process of secularization *"fere ubique,"* "almost everywhere."

## Life and Science and the Emerging Eugenic Society

The USA is moving toward an eugenic society wherein "perfection" lies in the possession of a set of perfect chromosomes and genes. The drive to eliminate the "defectives" has taken on mammoth proportions; bioethics has become a byword, but often a word without true ethical, moral or religious roots. The drive to control and manipulate man is no myth. It moves on relentlessly in its mechanistic view of man.

The poor, the aged, the sick, the unborn, the insane, the desperately ill, the defectives, the radically different—those without that set of perfect chromosomes, beware! The traditional protections have been eroded in the name of science and humanity. Joseph Fletcher, the prophet of "situation ethics," may well be cited to illustrate: "If we are morally obligated to put an end to a pregnancy when amniocentesis reveals a terribly defective fetus, we are equally obliged to put an end to a patient's hopeless misery...."

It is proxy judgment! Big Brother knows best!

## The Control of Human Potential

To control through eugenics the type of human being born is the goal of human engineering. The human race can be programmed by a variety of methods: the selection of special genetically "superior" donors of sperm and ovum; artificial insemination, a most beneficial technique in the production of domestic animals; the yet-to-come nuclear transplantation or "cloning," and other methods, to screen out "undesirable genes." Pregnancies can be monitored; defectives eliminated. It is fabrication of man by man!

## The Control of Human Behavior

New techniques have been developed to control the behavior of human beings, with, it should be stated, very questionable effectiveness and success. Neurobiologists and psychosurgeons have implanted micro-electrodes in the brain; employed electrical stimulation; used drugs in an effort to modify memory, check aggressive behavior, sedate "libido," and even affect intelligence. It is the domestication of man!

## Technology and Man, the Dehumanization Process

Technology, as well as science, has been a great boon to man: it too promises even greater blessings and benefits. Yet the threat of abuse casts its shadow, and the moral implications challenge man to control this leviathan before it controls man. Through the marvels of electronics and communications with the speed of sound and light, the people of the earth have been brought closer together, closer to realizing that all live on one limited planet. At the same time, these powers can and are fast becoming means of spying, surveillance, eavesdropping, and a general invasion of personal and corporate privacy. The fundamental human right to be secure in person and free from inordinate prying and snooping into private life and personal affairs now stands in danger of rapid erosion.

No wonder that Alexander Solzhenitsyn cried out in protest: "We took a marvel of nature...interfering with the most perfect thing on earth, namely man, and turned it into a stone. I can already hear the boots stamping down the corridors." (Candle in the Wind)

## Single Identifying Number, as a Dehumanizer

Even more insidious and ominous, because it touches the general population, is the abuse of computers and data banks. Governments are constantly seeking to put numbers on citizens, for the purpose of regulation. The urge to label each person at birth with a lifelong number, with a single identifying number, has already tempted many nations, including the USA where so far it has been resisted successfully.

Private industries too, such as banks, insurance companies, and credit bureaus, have been keeping master files on all who do business with them, storing all manner of personal data in central data banks, thanks to that many-splendored animal, the electronic computer, which never forgets and is incapable of forgiving. It is man becoming a number!

Again Solzhenitsyn: "The time will come when computers can be programmed to deliver human happiness and social justice. The price is merely our freedom."

The descriptions given above are not science-fiction. Large segments of major forces in the USA are committed to a planned eugenic society. This new society, if fashioned along the specifications of science and technology unrestrained by truly human and humane considerations, will be essentially, inherently anti-Christian and anti-human.

There is arising a *secular* answer which denies basic human dignity and freedom. This "secular" answer will no doubt be promoted as will the role of the USA in its export of moral and ethical conclusions propounded in the name of "science" and "applied science."

Much stress has been placed on the classes of people, whether rich, middle-class, poor, and the destitute; on the economy under which they live; on the type and form of government—whether Communist, Socialist, monarchy, democracy, or variations thereof—which rules these people. But the picture will be gravely deficient if it does not take into account man in his emerging society so deeply influenced by science, especially the life sciences, and technology.

Not only Western man, but his brother in the Orient have fast become creatures of the science and technology that serves them: perhaps they are even a bit mesmerized by the rapid advances of medicine and space travel, to mention just two. The miracle of radio and television, unknown to ancestors, even kings and presidents, has become a universal tool of instant world-wide awareness, in remote villages as well as in palaces.

Similarly, commerce and trade among nations involve much more than the sharing of goods and materials, more than political strategies. With its products and resources goes a country's economics, politics, human values, culture, religion and civilization.

## Conclusion

The increased autonomy of the secular, of science, and technology, does not negate religion; indeed, the religious dimension still fascinates man. Modern man is restive in his new world as he sees the depth and quality of life sacrificed to technological achievement and material abundance. He doubts a scientific Utopia or even the possibility of one; he reflects on the wars and oppression of the 20th century and remains skeptical.

The Church looks to affirming not only that God is not dead nor irrelevant, but that God lives and is faithful. The Church must demonstrate that it too lives and is faithful in spite of the adverse currents of history in any age or epoch. The Church must proclaim the dignity of man by reason of the Incarnation, and the great value in nature because of its creation by God.

The Church faces a great opportunity to penetrate the new insights into man and creation; to cooperate with scientists, making clear her disinterested concern for man, for his progress, and yet further mastery of the mysteries of the natural world. The Church must express her belief that she never fears science or technology and sees neither as necessary threats to revealed religion, precisely because the Church believes in the unity of all truth since God is its source.

Science and technology, on the other hand, need the moral experience and ethical intuition of the Church. The on-going destruction of defective man (men and women) *by other men;* the fabrication of man *by other men;* the domestication of man *by other men;* the invasion of man in his private life by reduction to a specific number, *by other men,* challenge not simply ethical principles but the deepest dogmatic and doctrinal truths. C. S. Lewis has remarked "man's victory over nature is really man's victory over man using nature as a vehicle" *(Abolition of Man,* p. 69).

The conception that science is an independent body of knowledge, coldly objective without any cultural bias of its very own; that science is the means par excellence of conquering social problems and creating a utopia on earth through inevitable evolution and progress is itself a cultural bias.

There is a breakdown of communication between laymen and scientists. The general public often accepts scientific authority with blind reverence, as almost religious in nature.

Scientists, in turn, often reject the unifying philosophical themes, the underlying human values in their research, ignoring the social consequences of their ideas. Not only does the common man appeal to science for justification, but even the Communist cites the *scientific* principles of Karl Marx; the psychoanalyst, the *scientific* principles of Sigmund Freud—a use of the concept of "science" in a very broad and indeed unverifiable way.

The "secular" defends itself in its own cultural bias, invoking "the scientific" and "the technological." It threatens to dehumanize the human race.

# CHAPTER SEVEN

## THE RELATIONSHIP OF SCIENCE AND UNBELIEF

> "Indeed it happens in many quarters and too often that there is no proportion between scientific training and religious instruction: the former continues and is extended until it reaches higher degrees, while the latter remains at elementary level."
>
> John XXIII, *Pacem in Terris,* no. 153

Science, with its partner technology, has had a most profound influence on religion. Some scientific theories, moreover, have been destructive of traditional beliefs, yielding a strong bias towards unbelief, religious indifference, agnosticism, and atheism. With its marvelous achievements, science has become the "miracle" worker of the present dispensation, able to explore the far-away planets and the internal DNA molecule, producing lightning communications and wonder drugs.

In somewhat of a paradox, man is made the measure of all things, quasi-omnipotent, a king in his own right, with no need of God or of transcendent moral restraints; and at the same time deemed a mere machine reducible in principle to the laws of physics and chemistry. Either way, the seeds of unbelief have been sown down through the years.

From the 18th century has come Newton's picture of man as machine and God as cosmic clockmaker; from the 19th century, Darwin's new idea of evolving man and divine imma-nence in a world of both chance and law; and from the 20th century, the proposition that science must be considered more as a method rather than as a content. Many modern philosophers, influenced by a positivism which extols science as the only norm for all discourse, reject religion as having no cognitive claims, no basis in truth.

But how much weight must be given to science in rela-tionship to unbelief? How great is a "profound influence," and how compared in importance to the secularization of contemporary society; its sex revolution; the atomic threat; the separation of the Church from both education and the political order; the recognized autonomy of intellectual disciplines; and the historical view of the 20th century as the most bloody in all human history?

Science must be accorded a very significant but by no means a solo role. It has been well said that "it is not the philosophers and scientists, but the greatest theologians of our time who are saying 'God is dead,' or that notions of 'God out there' are antiquated. These views are becoming popular" (Stark & Glock, *American Piety,* 1970, p. 206).

The intellectual heritage of modern man, one would be tempted to call it "baggage," contains within it the seeds of unbelief. It is the purpose here to trace some of these salient features in that heritage which have persisted to the present day. Moreover, an attempt will be made to give some of the evidence which measures the actual influence, insofar as it be possible, of science towards unbelief by way of the find-ings of sociologists.

## In the Field of Physical Science

Most, if not all, scholars agree that the work of Newton (1687) in physics gave the classical base for a conception of both nature and the nature of man. Although a religious man and believer himself, yet he laid the foundations for both determinism and materialism.

Nature was pictured by Newton as a closed, law-abiding machine; the cosmos was always predictable. Nature was an intelligently designed machine, following fixed canons, man included. God was the great clockmaker; and the world, once started, runs its course predictably and inevitably. Scientists in the 18th century *consciously* adopted the model of "man as machine" as the fundamental mode of understanding. This Newtonian paradigm was central to physics and science in general for the next two centuries.

Thus man himself was predictable in principle, and freedom and consciousness were "left-overs" from pre-scientific days.

That this basic notion perdures down through the centuries even to the present day may be illustrated by the 1981 television series in the USA called "Cosmos," featuring a leading astronomer, Carl Sagan, who had become a celebrity known to tens of millions as an attractive popularizer of science and its newest discoveries, especially the space probes to the planets.

Speaking to millions he said: "I am a collection of water, calcium and organic molecules, called Carl Sagan...but is that all?... Some people find this idea somehow demeaning to human dignity. For myself, I find it elevating that our universe permits the evolution of molecular *machines* as intricate and subtle as we are" *(Time,* Oct. 20, 1980).

The surprising fact is that this Newtonian concept of man-as-machine survives to the present day, even in spite of the advent of quantum physics which radically challenged the classical notions. Matter was no longer described solely as made of solid atoms and particles; there were electrons, X-rays, and radioactivity. Matter was seen to take on the nature of both particles and waves; predictability in significant measure was modified by the concept of probabilities, the principle of indeterminacy. The classical description of reality has given way to substantial modification, matter being seen to be more a sequence of events rather than a mere collection of substances.

Man-as-machine is not in any sense a literal picture of reality, nor even a useful fiction. Yet the machine model persists!

## In the Field of Philosophy

The British philosopher, David Hume (1776), laid the foundations for the systematic justification of scientific empiricism and religious agnosticism. Enthusiastically the French *philosophes* extended Newton's *Principia* and method in physics to nature. It was the Age of Reason.

Nature was understood to be pre-determined and could be reduced to simple elements. God at first was seen as "deist"; then through the eyes of skepticism; thence to materialism and avowed atheism. God became unnecessary. Man, however, was humanly perfectible through reason, and social progress possible only through science.

Baron d'Holbach summed up the *argumentum* in a bit of poetry:

> "Oh Nature! Sovereign of all beings!
> And you her adorable daughters,
> virtue, reason, and faith!
> Be ever our only Divinities."

Perhaps the most influential school in the years following was that of logical positivism. Its basic theses ran as follows: all propositions are either analytic or empirical. If analytic, then they are either tautological, i.e., a needless repetition of different words, or simply contradictory. In either case, the analytic yields no factual information. If empirical, then they are reports of sense experience, or generalizations from sense data, and truth emerges only from experimental verification. Metaphysics and theology yield only pseudo-propositions.

Auguste Comte (1857) added that positive science can and ought to perform the metaphysical and theological functions of former ages once fulfilled by religion. Similarly, Marxism affirmed not only that religion was the opiate of the people but also that God was simply a human projection. Lenin in 1916 said religion "is jejune idealistic nonsense with its origins in man's helplessness. We repudiate all morality which proceeds from supernatural ideas." In spite of the fact that Marxism was (and is) an ideology, and in no way "scientific'' in its principles, methods, and applications, yet it was and is seen by millions today as truly scientific, and accepted as such in many universities around the world.

The famous Vienna Circle (1930) brought the same doctrines to the present century. Its famous "verification principle" has been enunciated by Mach to the effect that all is sense knowledge, or compounds thereof which can be organized into a synthesis. There are no means to ends; there are no causes. Similarly Ayer: "all ethical judgment is purely 'emotive'; all utterances about the nature of God are nonsense. Hence atheism is just as meaningless as theism."

The evident rejection of metaphysics, whether by neo-positivism, linguistic analysis, atheistic existentialism or process philosophy, that is, the rejection of causality, fostered by a mechanical identification of cause and effect with absolute determinism in the universe, clearly postulated that there is no need for God or for faith or belief.

Nietzsche (1900) captured the implications well and clearly: "The greatest recent event that 'God is dead'; that the belief in the Christian God has become unbelievable, is already casting its first shadows over Europe.... We have all killed Him, you and I, all of us are His murderers."

In a somewhat similar vein, Cardinal Newman: "Things are tending to atheism in one form or another. What prospect does the whole of Europe present at this day...and every civilization through the world which is under the influence of the European mind?"

Ronald Butt, assistant editor, in the *Sunday Times* of London (1980) added this judgment on both the philosophers and Marxism:

"The characteristic philosophers of the 20th century, the intellectual contributions of the logical positivists and linguistic philosophers have tended, in their hostility to metaphysical propositions, to regard moral statements (being metaphysical) as nonsense.

"Likewise, Marxism with its root in the belief that man's material needs are the sole engine of history and in economic determinism, leaves little room in theory for moral concepts....

"Nevertheless, in the West, the influence of anti-metaphysical philosophers, of the Marxists, and other behaviorists have, all taken together, tended to fragment moral concepts into little more than human preferences" (*Human Life Review*, 1980, p. 6).

## In the Field of Life Sciences

Darwin (1859), like Newton before him but with more important results, "staggeringly so," as Robert Brungs has termed it, elaborated a new and distinctive world-view. He propounded a single unified scheme for both inanimate and animate nature in a dynamic and progressive process.

All nature is in flux, but always developing and constantly changing. All nature is a complex of interacting forces in mutual interdependence. Darwin suggested a new idea of immanence with both variations by chance and according to law. And finally, nature includes man and his culture; thus the animal ancestry of man implied that human culture could be analyzed in categories derived from biology.

The result was that the "theory" of evolution was appropriated and indeed misappropriated to almost every area of learning from astronomy, cosmology and biology through art and ethics to the social sciences. Ideas, institutions, cultures, and even religions were perceived to be "in evolution," and reducible to simple elements. Further, man and the human race were seen as inevitably in progress.

Julian Huxley, grandson of the great popularizer of Darwin, T. H. Huxley, and first Director General of UNESCO, still has described evolution as "blind and purposeless," with man being continuous with lower forms of life, even though unique. Evolutionary vision, he concluded, which is the naturalistic religion of the future, sees science as able to solve all problems.

Similarly, what is called "the New Religion" of sociobiology asserts that biology will absorb social sciences, humanities, and religion because all nature can now be seen to be reducible to genes, DNA, proteins and enzymes. "The basic laws of physical sciences are consistent with the laws of biological and social sciences, for this world has evolved from other worlds obedient to these laws...science is the only avenue to the understanding of reality" (E. O. Wilson, Harvard Univ., *The New Religion,* 1978).

Darwin then gave "a preliminary (on the level of species) unifying systematization" in the understanding of living systems. Today with the discoveries in genetics, particularly of the DNA structures, scientists have confirmed a new unity of nature, with no need to "depend on chance events to generate mutations essential for unravelling genetic phenomena."

Robert Brungs puts the matter in this wise: "We are developing an understanding of the basic unity of living systems at the level of the gene.... It is far too early to foresee all the implications of these new syntheses, but we can be absolutely certain that they will dwarf the results of any previous unitary understanding of the world."

Biological sciences are now the center of interest and development with "test-tube babies," surrogate mothers, cloning, euthanasia, contraception, abortion, genetic engineering, eugenics and population control. There will be a very significant impact on religion, morals and faith in three areas: personal dignity, personal freedom, and bodily integrity.

As the world enters the biotechnological age, as Brungs describes it, it finds itself rooted in a mathematical worldview, looking on all things—human beings as well—as essentially quantifiable and manipulable. Michael Zimmerman points out that "for contemporary mankind, *to be* means to be re-presented, or transformed and re-arranged, according to our desires and projects." Human beings are to be designed to fit specific activity rather than to fit activity to humans as they are. Thus the human being has no intrinsic purpose or destiny.

It would seem fair to conclude that the science of biology and its theory of evolution have become, for the modern mind, a world-view and philosophy unto itself. As extrapolated by many scholars, it too rejects both metaphysics and theology. Biology has been magnified into a comprehensive science comprising not only all natural sciences but as well all humanistic disciplines. Evolution has become a fundamental "law" of the whole material and cosmic process and the history of human culture, a philosophy rather than a scientific theory, and a firm base for unbelief since God is unnecessary in this world-view. It is in this context that the argument between evolutionists and creationists has been revived.

## Science as Method

In both scientific and popular literature it has become commonplace to contrast science and religion as to method. It is the pressure point between the two, questioning the objectivity of each and its claim to validity, reality, and ultimately of truth.

"In the 19th century Darwin's theory of evolution encouraged new interpretations of divine immanence in the cosmic process, as well as naturalistic philosophies of man's place in the world of law and chance.

"But in the 20th century, the main influences of science on religion have come less from specific theories—such as quantum physics, relativity, astronomy, or molecular biology—than views of science as method" (Barbour, *Myths Models and Paradigms*, p. 2).

Science is perceived as rendering knowledge upon which all men can agree because it is objective, value-free, verifiable, both in content and method, and of universal validity. Religion is characterized as subjective, more emotive, of some use in society especially by way of personal commitment. Being non-cognitive, religion can lay no claim to reality nor to truth. Some would discount it further to the reductionist view that religion is the product of the interior forces of human psychology or the exterior forces of society.

In the *Future of an Illusion* Freud described religion in purely psychological terms as human projections in what could be described as neurosis. Comte rejected metaphysics in favor of positivist science. Sociology would in effect become just another form of scientific knowledge verifiable by sense data.

Religious beliefs *de facto* do serve as the basis and motive for personal identity and growth, as a creative force. Religion cannot be confined to guilt, anxiety, and emotional responses, to the destructive effects of maladjustments, to psychological responses, as Freud would have it.

Similarly, sociology can empirically investigate the functions of religion and beliefs in society, authority and value structures without confining religion to social functions, as Comte would have it.

Yet the positivist principle itself has proved too narrow, too purblind, even for science, since it effectively excluded conclusive verification or proof of scientific theories.

Some modern scholars would see Descartes' methodical or systematic doubt as a truly scientific tool, somewhat inimical to religion and belief based on revelation. Others would go further and espouse a radical skepticism. Neither is intrinsic to science.

Belief does not rule out critical reflection nor a search for truth. But if science is perceived as alone producing valid knowledge, and precisely because of its "objective" methods, then the basis for unbelief is clearly laid.

The Second Vatican Council *(Gaudium et Spes,* no. 57) recognized the problem involving method: "No doubt today's progress in science and technology can foster certain exclusive emphasis on observable data, and an agnosticism above everything else. For the methods of investigation, which these sciences use, can be wrongly considered as the supreme rule for discovering the whole truth.... Yet the danger exists that man, confiding too much in modern discoveries, may even think he is sufficient unto himself."

## From Physical and Life Science to Human Science

With such an intellectual and scholarly heritage in Western civilization wherein the reductionist image of man as a complex machine reducible to simple elements and whose whole existence, it is asserted, can be exhaustively explained by the laws of physics and chemistry, it is no small wonder that science in its many-splendored forms suggests unbelief. Astrophysics will explain the origins of the universe; biochemistry, the origins of life; genetics, all organic evolution; paleontology will re-construct human ancestry. Religion's insistence that each human being is a genuinely unique and noble occurrence, that God is the source of all being—rather than that God is dead—is seen to be utterly irrelevant. It is an easy and valid assumption then, that science can be and has been used as a basis for unbelief. "A sky empty of angels becomes open to the intervention of the astronomers, and eventually the astronaut" (American Piety, 1970, p. 206).

But the question is fairly posed: with all of this scientific heritage, with its methods of radical doubt institutionalized at most universities, with its spirit and ethos appearing incompatible with the Judeo-Christian tradition, is it true that science actually promotes unbelief? And if so, to what degree?

To turn to sociology and to measurement of attitudes and opinions is to turn from the exactness and precisions of both the physical and life sciences. Yet the results are, at present, the best science can render with all the caveats and conditions annexed thereunto. Sociologists approach the questions with their own discipline which is neither the methods of physical or life sciences, nor of history or philosophy. Sociology is a "human science," people oriented; and since the human being and human race are involved, it cannot fulfill the canons of experimental science in their simplicity, predictability, and reproducibility. But, what light can it shed?

## In the Field of Sociology

There is no doubt that science, in its many-faceted forms, has been a basis for unbelief. Moreover, it has been a cherished dogma that science is a truly secularizing agent in society, inimical to religious affiliation and belief. Sociologists have endeavored to measure the relationships between religion and science as they affect the general public, university students, and university professors. They seek relationships, as revealed through statistical measurements, between science and scientists with religion and church membership, and with believers and non-believers.

Most sociological research in the USA begins with the conclusion of World War II as most convenient and rich in potential.

## The General Population, USA

The religious profile of the general population in the USA gives some indication of trends towards belief and unbelief.

Of the people in the USA (1970), 97% said that they believe in God: Protestants with *no doubt* 71%; Catholics 81%; with 17% added to the Protestant total "with some doubt," and 13% Catholic "with some doubt." Atheism as such is not popular. As to the divinity of Christ as the Son of God, 69% of American Protestants, and 86% of Catholics affirmed their belief. For life-after-death, 89% of Protestants and 91% of Catholics answered in the affirmative.

In the matter of church attendance and church affiliation for all Americans, there have been cyclical changes in approximately five-year segments. Age played a major role: In 1960, 46% of American adults, 21 years to 29, attended church weekly; in 1970 only 28%; in 1975 up to 34%. For the age group 30-49, the figures were 49%; 47%; and 44% respectively. For 50 years and over: 47%; and in 1975, 49% (Hoge: *Social Factors*, p. 21). Catholics showed a similar trend: in 1975, the youngest group 45%; middle group 57%; oldest group 68% at weekly Mass.

The divorce rate in the USA rose alarmingly from 1962 where there were 10 divorces for each thousand married women, 1970—15 per thousand, and in 1975—19 per thousand. Similarly, after 1969 there was a sharp increase in the acceptance of abortion in the general population.

As for Catholics, they are reported as approving premarital sex between engaged couples: 12% in 1962; 43% in 1975; approving remarriage after divorce 52% in 1963 to 73% in 1975. A recent study by Dean Hoge of Catholic University (1981) shows that there are virtually no converts to the

Catholic faith from the secular culture. Over 90% are received into the Catholic Church from a culture already Christian.

Science is not so much as mentioned as a factor among the USA general population:

"Changes in church commitment are part of a broader pattern of value changes. *All data support this view.* Other areas in the overall cluster undergoing changes are attitudes about sex and family, birth control, ideal family size, civil liberties, legalization of marijuana, and (among Catholics) political party identification.

"In all these areas, change since the 1950's has taken the same pattern. It has been the direction of individualism, personal freedom, and tolerance of diversity" (Hoge, *Church Growth & Decline,* 1978).

The *direct* influence of science on the general population seems minimal, and is not shown by the research to be a major factor in belief or unbelief. But in educated circles, which may well have an enormous *indirect* effect on the general public, the secular humanistic world-view, based on the American scientific and intellectual establishment, rooted in the universities, takes on a much greater significance.

## University Students

The intense alienation of youth in the 1960's was a phenomenon of all Western civilization. Both the Church and religion, on the one hand, and the secular humanistic culture with its scientific and technological skills were perceived to fail the youth of the world. The secular culture failed to give a personal meaning to life, little about authentic human community, which fact gave rise to new religious movements with sensitivity sessions, transcendental meditation, Eastern mystical movements, evangelical sects, fundamentalist cults and communes. Students were at the heart of these drastic changes.

In 1960 in a study of twelve universities, 100% of both Catholics and Protestants under 25 affirmed belief in God; 98% of those over 25 years of age. Of the graduate students about 25% said they had no religious affiliation, while another 25%

said they attended church every week. Students majoring in the Arts and Sciences reported that 95% of them were raised as Protestants or Catholics; only 75% still practiced their faith. But Protestants lost 16%, Jews 4%, and Catholics 1% of this total (Greeley).

On the other hand, in September 1980, freshman students (18-19 years old) at the University of California and Stanford considered themselves more conservative than their predecessors, an increase of 5% from four years previously. Only 2% considered themselves "far left," while 43% called themselves middle-of-the-road politically.

But over 25% said they had no religious preference, 13% were reborn Christians. 75% favored legalized abortion; and almost half, legalized marijuana. 66% said that their career and job training was as important as an education and noted the importance to be successful financially *(San Francisco Chronicle,* Feb. 5, 1981).

In a national survey of French students of sociology in the faculties of Letters and Human Sciences (June 1965) Marxism was the theory supported by the largest single group, 35% of all polled. In Shanghai, in Fuden University (September 1980), the students answered that 33% believed in communism, 25% in fate, 25% in "nothing," and a very few in Christianity *(New York Times,* Jan. 20, 1981).

In a similar vein and with widespread sampling, American students entering universities—both men and women—with "no religious preference" comprised 10% of the class in 1968; 14% in 1971; 11% in 1974; 9% in 1977; and 8% in 1979—showing a trend back towards belief after the turbulent years in the 1960's and early 1970's (Astin cited by Hoge, 1979).

On being asked whether they need some religious orientation or belief, USA students showed a drastic drop from 1948-1979, the low point being in the 1960's, with a very slight upturn towards belief and orthodoxy in the 1970's. In attitudes towards science, the more religiously orthodox tended to see no conflict between religion and science, whereas in the 19th century, the more orthodox tended clearly to see the conflict and wished to discredit modern science. Religious liberal students argued that science must prevail over religious views; conservatives argued that, properly understood, there is no conflict (Hastings & Hoge, 1979).

"The volatility of college students seems to result from their greater independence from institutional commitments and their greater proximity to intellectual life. They seem the forerunners for cultural change generally. Cultural diffusion in the USA runs from college students to other youth and the general population" (Yankelovich, 1974:10).

Directly to the question of the alleged conflict of science and religion, Yinger reported that university students responded *affirmatively* to the following inquiries:

|  | 1946 | 1968 |
| --- | --- | --- |
| "Religion and Science support each other": | 21% | 22% |
| "The Conflict between Religion and Science is Negligible": | 32% | 34% |
| "The Conflict between Religion and Science is Reconcilable": | 17% | 15% |
| "The Conflict between Religion and Science is Irreconcilable": | 16% | 6% |

Thus only a minority of university students see themselves as caught between science and religion. One wonders whether or not a similar conclusion may be drawn about students as about professors, namely, that they can either easily integrate their scientific work with religious beliefs, or keep the two in parallel lines, separate in the practical world.

Julian Huxley (1953) asserted that the great majority of students fully accept the universal principle of natural selection as the sole agency of major evolutionary changes. Both scientists and sociologists would question this assumption.

Dr. Steven Muller, president of John Hopkins University in Baltimore, stated that: "The biggest failure in higher education today is that we fall short of exposing our students to values.... This situation has come about because the modern university is rooted in the scientific method, having essentially turned its back on religion" *(U.S. News,* Nov. 10, 1980). Here again there lies the suggestion that science has perhaps a very much greater influence *indirectly* than directly on belief or as the source of unbelief. Science may well have great influence directly on those other factors which do have the deepest effect on belief.

Yet Hastings and Hoge, the sociologists, insisted in 1981 that "Religious attitudes and commitments are brought to the university, not produced or measurably altered by the university experience."

## University Professors

University professors are less traditionally religious in both belief and practices than the general population, although it is not proven whether the results come from university training itself, or merely that people who do not hold traditional beliefs gravitate more to universities. All studies from 1931-1981 agree on this point.

In 1969, 80% of USA professors subscribed to some religion, with therefore one in five having no professed religious belief (Faia, *Social Analysis,* 1976, no. 37).

Yet 63% of 51,204 professors of *physical science* surveyed in 1974 said they were "open" to religion. 75% of scientists were affiliated with some church. Professors in physical sciences were more religiously inclined than those in the Humanities and social sciences. Those in disciplines closer to religion or with religious content in them like sociology, psychology, humanities, etc., were more influenced to leave religion than the professors in physical sciences.

Hoge and Keeler (1976) concluded that:

"The simple but widely held view of 'science vs. religion,' saying that science displaces commitment, cannot be sustained in view of the research, especially since scholars in the more rigorous natural sciences are generally more traditionally religious than scholars in the social sciences and humanities."

The cherished view, then, that science is the primary secularizing agent inimical to belief has not much direct support from the sociologists. There is little evidence that science has become a substitute for religion, "science as religion" as a functional equivalent to and competitor with traditional belief.

The strongest predictors of the belief and church affiliation of the university professors were not found in the fact that they studied science, nor in the number of years of their study of science. There was no correlation observed that the more science the less religion or, vice versa, the more religion the less science. Rather, the highest and truly significant correlations were found with early childhood religious beliefs and practices and the culture of the family and home. These strong forces, non-cognitive in many ways, were found to be little influenced by intellectual training. Religious commitments were strongly related to personal identity, sex roles, and family traditions. Religious beliefs were touched only to a limited degree by high-level academic and scientific work.

Sociologists, for example, devised what they call a "Faith in the Beneficence of Science Index." 56% of scientists surveyed agreed with the statement that "Modern science has now provided us with the ability to solve age-old problems of man and society." But only 32% agreed that "by the application of modern science can we master human evolution and direct human destiny." The significant fact here, however, is that there was *no* correlation found between faith in religion and faith in science. Again the predictors were to be found in home, family, life-style, and early culture. The strong non-cognitive sources were little disturbed by science.

A majority of scientists (university professors), according to Lemert, seem quite capable of either integrating their scientific work with their religious beliefs, or of keeping the two almost entirely separate in the practical world. Modern consciousness, he suggests, is quite able to sustain dissonance between religious and scientific norms.

Sociologists maintain that science is not in the business of destroying religion or undermining beliefs. Social factors are much more influential than scientific ones. Greatest impact on belief and unbelief comes from the area of family life—including sexual behavior, marriage, child-rearing and family life-style. Other social changes, including race relations, economic well-being, occupation, business, and international politics, have less effect. Higher cognitive factors such as philosophy, science, or literary intellectual life are perceived as even less influental (Hoge, 1980).

Demographic changes do not explain erosion from belief. The negative trends towards belief and religion are not explicable by migration, urbanization, use of leisure time, the birthrate, or standard of living.

The *indirect* effects of science on unbelief may be postulated by assessing the *direct* effects of science precisely on family life, sexual behavior, marriage, changing social and political structures and economic affairs. Such data are not at hand.

But it seems clear that the great debate of the 1980's will be "the affirmation of culture versus withdrawal from culture," with such topics as materialism, personal morality, limits to growth, and social and political responsibility as primary.

## Conclusion

Into the last two decades of the 20th century, men and women carry and support a cultural heritage deeply informed and permeated profoundly by science and its daughter, technology. This scientific inheritance has been basically quite congenial to unbelief, and as well quite destructive of traditional religious belief and faith.

Man was made the measure of all things, his progress and indeed perfectibility inevitable and inexorable with the force of evolution; his origins explicable, his future to be secure, given time. He was desacramentalized, even as his body lost its sacramentality, its nature as something sacred. Newton and Darwin, Hume and Comte, Marx and Freud, as well as their popularizers Huxley and Sagan, laid premises for modern denials of man as a creature made to the image and likeness of God. With the rejection of metaphysics, the floodgates were open to theories and hypotheses, more or less plausible, that laid the foundations for the erosion of the intrinsic dignity and worth of each man, woman, and child, born or unborn. Bodily integrity itself is imperiled.

Yet this heritage has not been homogeneous by any means. Twentieth century man has lived in the bloodiest of centuries. This century with its wars and exquisite tyrannies, made possible in large measure by science and technology in the hands of *"perfectible man,"* has made men and women raise questions that look to a moral order, to further judgment where applied science touches the human race. Science has not produced either the Utopia promised nor the liberation predicted so confidently in the name of evolutionary progress. Even scientists, in two very notable circumstances and predicaments, called for ethical considerations over and above the scientific.

The first happened when President Truman was deciding to drop the first atom bomb on Japan; the second, when DNA was discovered and its potential dangers surmised. On both occasions, leading scientists questioned the morality of what was contemplated. For the first time in history, the USA scientists agreed to a voluntary moratorium on DNA research, joined by British men and women of science.

Moreover, the new sciences are not uncritically accepted by the men and women of today, conditioned by the disappointments of recent history. The potential for good in nuclear energy is countered by the menace of bombs and warfare of cataclysmic proportions, if not simply by radioactive poisoning. The blessings of the genetic and biomedical revolutions are tempered by the horrible manipulations and gross experimentations that are reducing human beings to utterly expendable things, objects, brute matter. Freud and Marx, as scientists, have seen better days; so today's observer accepts the promises and dogmas of the popularizers and prophets with some of the skepticism, or perhaps a methodical doubt, which they themselves have preached. The "Gospel of Progress" clearly needs a new hermeneutic and exegesis.

Modern men and women do not naively accept the "miracles" of science and technology, even though deeply influenced by them. The electronic revolution with all-pervasive television extending more and more towards every household in the world; the computers and data banks; space exploration and inter-planetary travel; the genetic revolution with the promises of recombinant DNA, are all received with something of a sophistication lacking in the 19th or earlier 20th century man.

Men and women of the last two decades of the 20th century simply do not accept the notion, sown in early days, of the inevitability of progress in the human race. History has been a hard task-master in this century. The reasons are not far to seek:

"When a divine substructure and the hope of eternal life are wanting, man's dignity is most lacerated, as current events often attest. The riddles of life and death, of guilt and grief, go unsolved, with the frequent result that men succumb to despair.

"Meanwhile, every man remains to himself an unsolved puzzle...especially when life's major events take place" (Gaudium et Spes, no. 21).

Science has indeed laid the groundwork for unbelief, religious indifference, agnosticism, and atheism, perhaps more indirectly than commonly thought. Yet unbelief shows much more direct correlation with factors other than science.

The presence of evil in the world, the precepts of a moral law, especially in reference to sexual morality including marriage, divorce, contraception, abortion, homosexuality, pornography, etc.; the secularization of social, educational and political structures; a general moral decline with world-wide terrorism and materialism; the autonomy of various disciplines, are seen to correlate more positively with unbelief than science and technology.

This climate which encourages religious indifference has been dubbed neo-paganism of a somewhat Nietzschean hue, affecting morality and "clearing the way for a return to pagan naturalism...fomenting the secularizing of moral standards...(for) when you do not live the way you think, you end up thinking the way you live" (Archbishop Poupard, Fifth Synod of Bishops, Oct. 1980).

The research is not at all conclusive, however. Perhaps there is a much greater influence than the scientists and the public-at-large perceive. It seems probable, at least, that science and technology have exerted their influential pressures through the very factors themselves such as secularization, morality, life-style and the like, and thereby contribute indirectly through them to a fostering of unbelief and agnosticism. The testimony of scholars and experts would suggest even a more direct relationship; the research data would mitigate their judgment.

There is no necessary relationship between science and unbelief; nor scientific methods. Over the years science, while congenial to agnosticism, has seen itself co-opted for purposes and ends decidedly un-scientific, whether for social, political, economic, or ideological purposes. Science is not as objective, value-free and as disinterested as some theologians postulate; and religion is not as subjective, value-laden, and passionate as some scientists might assume. Both can be true as well as useful to mankind since they share a common source, namely, God.

Pope St. Leo the Great (461) perhaps summed up the matter best when he spoke on the dignity of man in relation to nature:

"Wake up, man, and recognize the high estate of your human nature. Remember, you are made in God's image, and that, though defaced in Adam, the image has been restored in Christ.

"Use creatures as they should be used: the earth, the sea, the sky, the air, the springs and the rivers....

"Far be it from us, beloved, to bid you scorn God's works, or think that what God created can be contrary to your faith, for the good God has Himself made all things good."

# CHAPTER EIGHT

## THE TALE OF TWO COUNTRIES

> "For it is indeed clear that the Church
> has always taught and continues
> to teach that advances in science
> and technology and the prosperity
> resulting therefrom are truly to be
> counted as good things and regarded
> as signs of the progress of
> civilization."
>
> John XXIII, *Pacem in Terris,* no. 246

There has always been a streak of naiveté in the American soul. World War I was to end all wars with open covenants openly arrived at; World War II was to end all wars because of the frightful role of science and technology with the very real threat of atomic annihilation. In somewhat the same vein, Americans refuse to see any similarities between the conditions and practices which led up to the Holocaust in Central Europe and what are being espoused in the brave new world forty years later. Yet the exercise in comparison cannot but have some sobering effects and call for deep reflection. Hence the "Tale of Two Countries."

Pius XII wrote that "The moral history of a nation is much more important than its scientific history." This theme must needs rest on some definite premises—four at least—before "The Tale of Two Countries" makes sense.

The first premise attests to the unity of all men. The world is a community and all human beings are brothers and sisters. All belong to the same family, and therefore an unjust threat to the liberty of one person, of one group, of one nation, of one race, or of one classification of people is indeed a threat to the liberty of all.

Secondly, religion and faith in no sense are a substitute for reason and knowledge in science; they must not intrude into the processes of science; they have no place there as such. By the same token science, in place of faith and religion, cannot define human values. There must be a mutual relationship and a very healthy one, but it is not a case of one substituting for the other.

Thirdly, science and technology can be demonic but not because they of themselves are evil. In a radical sense they are neutral. Abused in the hands of evil men, they can become and have become demonic in our society. But the conclusion is not that science and technology should be suppressed, curtailed, much less rejected, but rather should be transformed, sublimated, and engaged in the service of mankind if not under the fathership of God, at least they should be used in the service of our fellowmen. Otherwise, abused, they can and have become demonic instruments.

Fourth, mankind must look to the future with hope. It must not put its trust in the world of material abundance—abundance for everybody, that somehow it will be able to create a perfect society. No, this cannot successfully be man's purview. Rather it is a fact of history that there is sin in the world, that there is injustice in the world and consequently there will always be a struggle—a struggle for justice, for human liberty, a struggle for freedom. Mankind, as someone has very well remarked, is on a pilgrimage, not a vacation. It is a pilgrimage here on earth struggling in history to overcome injustice, to build the brotherhood of mankind. God is both the Alpha and Omega of that pilgrimage.

Having stated the premises, it is simple to recite a number of facts; to be overwhelmed by the facts themselves, horrendous as they prove to be. Yet the facts must be seen in their dynamism, in their motion, in their process. Where are they leading? Where have they led? Do they depict a trend or a process or a motion in history? They are to be examined to discover whether it is rational to say that from these very small beginnings come growth and results not intended, but which with time will become acceptable. Will good intentions —the improvement of the human race, the elimination of defective genes, the subjugation of disease and the abolition of poverty—and many other very good things cover over the question of the means used?

Are the good resolutions, the good desires, and the good intentions sufficient? Will we conclude that perhaps at times history has seen a touch of the demonic, a touch of real hell, because of the actions taken in the name of good intentions? Is the human race of the last quarter of the 20th century working with or interpreting properly the signs of the times? Is mankind, as Pope John XXIII suggested, really reading the signs of the times? The signs of the times of the brave new world of science? The "Tale of Two Countries" affords a basis for something of an answer.

The first country history described as a land of gifted people, of bright people, a land of geniuses, of saints and scholars, of scientists and workers. It is a land of literary giants— Schiller, Goethe, and Thomas Mann; a land of music and musicians—the three B's: Bach, Beethoven, Brahms, of Mozart and Schubert; and a roster of others ranging all the way from the heavy music dramas of Richard Wagner to the lilting operettas of the Strausses, Von Suppe, and of Lehar in Vienna—performers and composers without equal in any country. And in science this land has produced a veritable Who's Who of the pioneers: in physics Ohm, Roentgen, Steinmetz, Einstein, Meitner, Planck, and Bunsen; in medicine, Gerhard Domagk, the discoverer of miracle drugs, who opened up the whole new era of antibiotics; the land of Wasserman, Hahnemann, and Erlich; in architecture, the country of the gothic of Cologne and the baroque of Munich, the rococo of the Bavarian countryside.

It is a country of genius, but above all, it is a country of culture and it is civilized. And yet several decades ago its leaders were brought before the court of justice in Nuremberg and convicted of crimes against humanity, crimes against human nature.

The question here is very simple: what does history show about this most civilized country falling into what is conceded to be the demonic, the mad, the bizarre, the most unbelievable crimes against humanity? History tells that from very small beginnings on the ideas of purity of race; with good intentions to eliminate defective genes in future generations and to get rid of disease; with the concept of purity of blood which would enhance the quality of life and eliminate human defects, an ideology grew and waxed strong. The Master Race became canonized. In medicine and law a corollary was also born: the concept of worthless life.

With putative good intentions, using science, particularly genetics in justification, and the new tools of technology, the attack on life began. There are four major areas. The first was the most defenseless: the unborn of undesirable origins. The second in this evolution moved to experimentation on people "who really didn't matter any more"—people whose lives were really over, people who were sick, people who were defective. They were now ready to be experimented upon because they were now under the concept of "worthless life." No longer an asset to the state; no longer able for production; no longer good in themselves, they could at least serve science and future generations as experimental guinea pigs. The third area was euthanasia—aimed chiefly at the defective and the aged, the prototypes of "worthless life." The justifying ideology spawned, finally, genocide, the horrible slaughter of the Jewish people; the genocide of the Polish people; and the genocide of the Russian people—twelve million in all in murder camps and pogroms. The history of the camps of extermination tells that these three races and people stood on the lowest rung of the ladder to be exterminated as worthless life. And, even the very concept—in German called *Endlösung,* meaning "the end solution," the liquidation invoked in the name of scientific progress toward a master race, toward purifying the blood, toward progress for the future, grew into a national ideology.

At the end of the War, the second country sent its own prosecutor, Robert Jackson, to Nuremberg to act as prosecutor of the leaders of the National Socialist regime, an American to draw up the indictment. It accused the leaders of the first country of four major crimes, the four just enumerated: abortion, experimentation on human beings, euthanasia and genocide.

The indictment took infinite pains to describe in detail how laws of all *civilized* countries, emphasizing civilized, repudate "the end solution." Read history; read law; read medicine; all civilization rebels. Then came the realization that these men in their defense would say, "But I was only following the laws of my own state. I was following the statutes promulgated by the Reichstag. I was following decisions that were agreed to by our Supreme Court." Justice Jackson's response was that regardless of all these excuses, they will be tried and convicted because as human beings, as rational creatures, they' have committed crimes against humanity. In Article IV of that indictment he asked the rhetorical question, "Does it take these men by surprise that murder is considered a crime?"

It was curious that such rhetoric would be an indictment. And yet this was the judgment, not only of the second country that had sent the prosecutor, but was indeed, the consensus of practically the entire world. The public media underlined the Judeo-Christian tradition and the pre-Christian Hippocratic Oath, with its strictures against abortion and the taking of unborn life; they cited with approval the United Nations with its Declaration of Human Rights including the right to life of the unborn, to human dignity and liberty; the Nuremberg Code with its same provisions. Later the Code of Helsinki would proscribe unjust human experimentation, stating that the doctor who is in charge of a human being must at all times be the protector of the life and the health of that person under experimentation.

Such was the reaction of world opinion; codes were drawn up now so that these things would never happen again. Surely as all men see these obvious crimes against humanity— surely, surely—these things would never happen again. It was not a case simply of *"Vae Victis!*—Woe to you who are conquered!" But even more *"Vae Victoribus*—Woe to you victors who sit in judgment lest you fall prey to exactly the same crimes."

Decades later, Americans are asking the same questions, very much in anguish as American citizens: what is the trend in our own times and in our own practices, in our own civilization? What are the signs of the times? What is the motion in history? They once sat in judgment on the German leaders and particularly, in a sense, the German nation. Are we on the same road or a similar road? When we talk about the attack on unborn life, where are we? Or with experimentation on human beings, where are we? Or euthanasia? Or genocide? These are at least fair questions.

The attack on life relied on semantics and euphemisms, many under the umbrella of a scientific "fact." After the U.S. Supreme Court decision on abortion, articles were published in which rather prominent people were reported to have said, "I see nothing wrong with getting rid of a piece of protoplasm." Failing that: "Well, after all, the unborn life is merely an organ of the mother, and there is no problem in the excision of an organ." But biologists and other scientists said that scientifically speaking there was an "organism." Another approach asserted that there are certain acts that are victimless crimes. Doctor Nathanson in New York, after he had presided over 60,000 abortions, in a reversal of thought and mind said, "You know, I think we are doing something wrong." As a scientist and physician, he added: "I think we are taking life." Perhaps that came from the number of abortions he had witnessed and where he saw life. But 60,000 abortions later he said, "I want no part of it. We are doing something here that we do not understand." His antagonists bitterly replied: "Oh, this isn't life, this is only potential life." Or—"We are not killing a fetus, no, we are merely interrupting a pregnancy." Or—"We are terminating a pregnancy." There are no real victims, the second country's citizens said; but they received fundamental support from a most powerful quarter.

The Supreme Court asserted: "The fetus, at most, represents only the potential of life." Now the majority members of the court based their decision on this remarkable assertion. Notice the words: "the fetus at most," not "at worst," or "at least," but "at most" not *is* but "represents." What does that mean? "Represents"—represents what? Here are semantic gymnastics. The problem is precisely that American education, American medicine, American law, and even much American theology, can hide behind words. Change the words, don't say what things are, and somehow the problem will be solved.

Euphemisms became the order of the day. Over one hundred years ago, in 1871, as a matter of fact, the American Medical Association in a court case was asked to express its opinion on the question of abortion. This case was cited (although not subscribed to) in the briefs of the Supreme Court decision of 1973. After studying the matter the American Medical Association of 1871 concluded: "We had to deal with human life. In a matter of less importance we could entertain no compromise," adding that: "...an honest judge on the bench would call things by their proper names,—we could do no less." The point was made that if they could accept no compromise on lesser things than the right to life, they could not do so by using deceptive euphemistic language to cover up the awful reality of the taking of innocent life. In the same wise in September, 1970, the California Medical Journal editorialized that "The very considerable semantic gymnastics which are required to rationalize abortion as anything but the taking of human life would be ludicrous if not often put forth under socially impeccable auspices." What has the prosecutor, the second country, to respond to the convicted first country some decades later?

The second area of the Nuremberg indictment concerned experimentation on human subjects. The cases are legion. The Tuskegee syphilis experiment, celebrated in a best seller in 1981 called *Bad Blood,* is a horror tale in American medicine. From 1932 to 1972 the U.S. Public Health Service conducted "a death watch" over some 443 men, almost all black, with the collaboration of public health and private doctors, both white and black, and local and state governments, and even draft boards.

In order to determine the true effect of social diseases, and without any care of the cost in suffering to the men and their families, these human subjects were never told that they had syphilis. They were given harmless "medicines" and allowed to suffer and die, even though antibiotic cures were readily available. The U.S. Surgeon General even sent letters of appreciation to 25-year survivors for their participation in the experimentation. One senior physician, as author James J. Jones reports in his book, wrote: "As I see it, we have no further interest in these patients until they die."

"When the Associated Press broke the story in 1972, a shocked public drew comparisons with the Nazi's Nuremburg experiments. Neither contrite nor apologetic, most of the study's senior physicians offered inadequate scientific defenses and improbable moral ones" (N.Y. Times, June 21, 1981). One doctor even added: "There was no racial side to this. It just happened to be in a black community." Might not the same defense have been used by the war criminals some years before? It just happened to be Jews at Auschwitz; and Russians at Belsen; and Poles at Dachau?

The U.S. Government settled claims out of court for ten million dollars.

But within a year of this publicity came another public outcry about the sterilization of two girls, aged 11 and 12. Their mother had signed a release form, but she signed with an X, because she was illiterate and utterly ignorant of what she was doing. Just a few months later, the Central Intelligence Agency's experiments, under the aegis of the U.S. government as in so many other cases, came under public scrutiny and disclosure.

In 1963 many people were given the hallucinogenic drug LSD without their knowledge. One family received word that their husband and father had thrown himself out of a hotel window in New York, apparently a suicide. His wife and children lived with this burden for many years. There was no word of the LSD given to the father by agents of the CIA without his knowledge or consent. Ten years later, the case made headlines on national TV: the U.S. government conceded its guilt without even a court trial. It cost the taxpayers slightly more than a million dollars in reparation to the family.

But the CIA was not alone in the government. A short news item on national TV informed the public that a Health, Education, and Welfare (HEW) study showed that 35% of the experiments on human beings have been conducted without the consent of the subject. In 50% of the cases no records had been kept, and in 74% of the cases the government rules had been violated. The United States government had assured that it has been strict in its regulations about all these things.

In 1974 the *Journal of Pediatrics* reported that twelve mothers had agreed to abortion. By reason of that fact the researchers said, "Well if they are already destined to be destroyed, we can use them for experimentation because for all practical purposes they are dead." They took the aborted fetuses and kept them alive artificially. To measure oxidation in the brain, they beheaded the fetuses and kept the heads functioning artificially. While done overseas, the experiment was reported at the American Medical Association's National Convention in San Francisco, and raised no public concern.

The HEW guidelines say that "in human experimentation we must always respect the human character of the fetus." Not the *character*, but the *human character* of the fetus, it states. The Supreme Court, however, stated in effect that the unborn have no rights, if the mother so decides. They can be killed at the will of the mother alone without the intervention of the State. What can the second country say to the first country on this matter?

The third area is euthanasia, where in the first country leaders were indicted and convicted of crimes against humanity. Are there certain people who are worth preserving, an elite? And others not worth saving who are to be done away with, be destroyed, because they really are not productive in society, or are its burden? Is it any different in the case of capitalism and of totalitarian socialism? The one says—after all, life is the survival of the fittest, let the others be damned; the other says—unless men and women are productive in terms of the State, they are "worthless life" and, really, the State has no interest in preserving them. It is a concept of the "life boat" ethic.

At least seventeen legislatures in the States of the USA have euthanasia proposals already. People now argue that there is a right *not* to live. A suicide pact—as in the case of those two famous Protestant leaders, husband and wife, the Van Dusens, who committed suicide together because they were sick, has been seen as a touch of glory. No one can judge them or their motives before God or even before man. But they were held up as something saintly because they did not wish to face the future. So they made a mutual suicide pact because now there is a "right" to die. Positively, to get rid of one's self!

The fourth area of genocide furnishes no compelling evidence in the USA, whether the extremes of war as in Vietnam or Cambodia, or the starving refugees around the globe. The road to holocaust does not appear to lead from or to the USA.

But what of the first country 25, 30, and 40 years later? This country per capita is probably the most prosperous country in the world. It has made a remarkable come-back, precisely because of the very qualities pointed out. They are people of genius, people who can work hard, people of culture, people of sophistication, of scientific knowledge, of medical know-how. They are strong in science, in medicine, and perhaps stronger in history. The phantoms of the past have not died.

On June 18, 1974, the legislature in Bonn passed a law which stated that in the first trimester, the unborn life might be taken. Thus was it by law established—the right to destroy, to "terminate pregnancy" up to three months. The legislation was appealed to the Supreme Court of West Germany.

On Feb. 25, 1975, in a five to two decision, the Supreme Court of West Germany responded. First, it stated that Germans had learned a lesson from history. We of all people, it said, should have learned that we cannot put to the state or to a political regime the right to decide life and death among its citizens: "We learned and we are reacting to the administrative measures taken by the National Socialist Regime— the so-called destruction of worthless life in solution and liquidation. We see the value of life and the nature of the State in a way completely contrary to the conception of a political regime in which individual life meant little, and which therefore acceptably abused this usurped right to decide on people's life and death." The Court said in effect: learn from history.

Then, the German Supreme Court moved to a second answer. It stated that it had studied scientific evidence, particularly the biological evidence. "Everybody has the right to life. According to affirmed biological, physiological knowledge, life in the sense of historical existence of the human individual doubtlessly is present fourteen days after nidation. The process of development beginning at the time is continuous, without any evident gaps."

Life is a process from conception until death, biology says so, physiology says so. And, therefore, the right to live is guaranteed to all those who are alive. Such was the *scientific* view of the German Supreme Court.

The Court moved to public policy: what should be the public policy of any state with reference to unborn life or reference to life itself? "The duty of the state to protect every individual is all-encompassing. It not only prohibits direct interference with unborn life by the state, a point which is obvious, but this duty forces the state to protect and even support this unborn life." Notice—"which is obvious, not only to protect it but to support it." Again, the Court continued: "human life is estimated to have the highest value in the constitutional system, a fact needing no explanation. It is the compelling basis of the dignity of man and is the precondition for all basic constitutional rights." So, the third answer is that just for good, constitutional, public policy, it is quite obvious that the German constitution covers the right to life of the unborn.

Fourthly, the Court addressed itself to the question of the mother's right to privacy, the area in which the German Supreme Court confronts the basic argument of the United States Supreme Court. Describing the mother and unborn relationship as unique and very precious, it continued, "Pregnancy is a part of the woman's privacy which is protected constitutionally. If the embryo [notice, it doesn't say fetus] would be regarded only as a part of the mother's organism, abortion would be in the sphere of private decision. But as the nasciturus—that which is about to be born—is an independent human being of itself protected by the constitution, abortion involves social implications which make it necessary to bring it under the regulatory power of the state."

The German Supreme Court was saying, in effect, if it were just protoplasm, if it were just an organ, if it were just a part of the mother, it could see the argument for privacy. But obviously it is not. Therefore, the matter concerns another human being. The state has a pre-emptive interest in supporting that life.

And finally, the Court's conclusion: "Abortion destroys definitely existing human life. Abortion is an act of homocide and until now was called in the Penal Code 'killing a fetus'— the new term, interruption of a pregnancy, cannot disguise the fact."

The Church believes that the moral history of a nation is much more important than its scientific history. When the history of the 20th century is written, all of the great triumphs of science, art, music, of the civilization of the first country will be put into the shadows because of its moral history in the National Socialist regime. It will be known, before all else, for its contempt for human life in its four major manifestations as delineated at Nuremberg.

The National Socialist regime under Adolph Hitler appealed to science, to genetics, in particular, to give undergirding to its distinction of race. Aryan and non-Aryan, superman and inferior man, transcendental anti-Semitism, were justified in the name of the science of eugenics. Professors in German universities were recruited to lecture on "the science of race." Research projects on Judaism and Jewry, an Institute of Research on Judaism and Jewry, with a library of 350,000 volumes, were established. "The little difficulty the Nazis had in founding their 'science of race' among so many German intellectuals and scientists forms a melancholy chapter in the history of this macabre period" (Flannery, *Anguish of the Jews* p. 214).

The words "science and scientist" were admittedly very loosely used, and indeed radically perverted by the Nazis, yet many people were deceived, perhaps even persuaded somewhat by the veneer of scientific "truth," scientific reasoning and method. The science of eugenics was invoked and perverted to give a patina of rationality to "the first large-scale experiment in genocide" in all of history.

The German Supreme Court considered it essential that the facts of modern science were quite relevant to its decision. These scientific facts and conclusions were clearly the foundation upon which moral and legal judgment was made. By contrast, the USA Supreme Court, in its decisions on the right to life and on allied issues, has tended to ignore science as basic material upon which to fashion judgment. There are numerous examples constituting perhaps a clear trend that semantic gymnastics and pious euphemisms are substituted for basic facts in all four fields delineated by the U.S. prosecutor at Nuremberg: abortion of innocent life; experimentation on helpless human life; the destruction of elderly human life; and "the final solution" of genocide. Do these facts not signal a moral decline and a cheapening of human life?

At the very least they do attest that science and technology have a profound relationship to moral values, to society's welfare, and to civilization. The fundamental problem perdures: the relationship of scientific progress and a eugenic society. The answer must include moral judgments, human values, and ultimately an ethic on life itself.

The "Tale of Two Countries" is not a comforting story.

# CHAPTER NINE

## WHOSE MORALITY WILL PREVAIL?

"Far be it from us, beloved, to bid
you scorn God's works or think that
what God created can be contrary to
your faith, for the good God has
Himself made all things good."
Pope St. Leo the Great (461)

The problems engendered in society with the rise and
progress of science and technology cannot be answered or
even addressed through one single discipline, one single field
of learning, one way of looking at the subject. Rather the
approach must needs be inter-disciplinary, with experts from
diverse disciplines, and even the general public from many
cultures and moral persuasions contributing to an answer.
Are we in danger of one group or discipline forcing its
assumptions, morality and its standards of conscience on the
rest? As pilgrims from diverse disciplines and disparate
convictions and cultures, whose concept of values, whose
perception of human life, for example, will assume ascen-
dancy in our society? Can there be no consensus?

It should be admitted that there *is* such a danger. Protestants, Catholics, Orthodox, Jews, Mormons, Moslems,
Hindus, Buddhists, agnostics, humanists, atheists don't agree
on many of the practices and beliefs of their fellow citizens.
There is no consensus on certain "blue laws": the matter of
playing games such as football and baseball on Sunday; box-
ing, bingo, liquor laws; gambling, horse racing, dog racing;
prohibition, birth control. Some atheists even seem to choke
on the matter of religious holidays. At the same time, society
often tolerates what most people—indeed, a vast majority—

would consider to be evil: prostitution in all of its forms, pornography, and the widespread abuse of alcohol and drugs, both legal and illegal.

The question, then, is rightly asked: Is there no limit? Are there no boundaries to toleration? Are there not some things *so* basic to humanity, *so* fundamental to our society that a true informed majority can agree on them? Or cannot civilized people affirm that certain propositions are *so* fundamental to our society that it cannot get along without them? One might well be that life is sacred, and, if there be objection that the statement sounds too religious, that life is of supreme value even though it is not an absolute? That there is no such valid a concept as that of "worthless life"? Is not the right to life fundamental, again even though not absolute?

History answers in the affirmative, namely, that civilization rests on the basic concepts of life, dignity, human value and human worth. History says "yes" to human freedom and true liberty as based upon a respect for human life.

Back in Old Testament times the Jewish people made a clear distinction between the sons of Abraham, which they considered themselves to be—and, indeed, were—and the sons of Noah. As sons and daughters of Abraham, the Jewish people observed the laws of the Torah, which comprise the first five books of the Old Testament. There were at least 360 laws to be observed, very detailed ordinances covering almost every facet of life. It would have been unthinkable to the Jewish people to insist that the Gentiles and the strangers in their land would observe the laws of the Torah.

However, the Talmud, the books of tradition, tells of the sons of Noah, those other members of the human race, and the laws to which they would be subjected within the boundaries of Israel. There were seven laws that applied to all. The first was a positive one, the observance of social justice, and the other six were strictures against idolatry, blasphemy, adultery, robbery, unjust bloodshed, and eating flesh cut from a live animal. This last injunction, incidentally, showed great respect for animal life. The rabbis in the Talmud taught that these seven laws of Noah were considered universal, applicable to all men, and were to be imposed on the Gentiles, the Goyim, even to the matter of the death penalty. They affirmed that the observance of these laws was not only an obligation but a privilege and that they were a reflection of divine love and providence for the human race. The observance of the Noachic Laws were the foundation of all society and all civilization and, indeed, were the antithesis of any narrow, sectarian or denominational point of view. The Jewish people were saying that in *these* seven areas all share a common humanity with all men, and, therefore, a common obligation to observe the sanctity and dignity of life.

Under the Noachic Law, both Jews and Gentiles were enjoined from destroying fetal life; procured abortion carried the death penalty (Sanhedrin 57b) and did so by citing Genesis to the effect that "Man was made in God's image, and whoever sheds a man's blood must shed his own blood in return" (9:6). Centuries later, Moses Maimonides recorded this same prohibition in his *Mishnah Torah* in 1180 A.D.

Not all Jews or Gentiles have accepted the Noachic tradition. Arguments among the Talmudic scholars over the centuries were almost identical to those of today: the fetus is an organ of the mother; the fetus is a limb of the mother, an organic part of the mother; the fetus may be deformed, does not have independent animation; the fetus must be viable; must at least have motion, etc. Modern biology since 1930 at the latest has laid to rest most of these arguments: There is no doubt scientifically where life begins.

The point, however, is that the Jewish people did regard certain deeds and human actions as moral or immoral irrespective of whether a person was Jew or Gentile:

"There are three (persons) who drive away the *Shekinah* from the world, making it impossible for the Holy One, blessed be He, to fix his abode in the universe and causing prayer to be unanswered... (The Third is) he who causes the fetus to be destroyed in the womb, for he destroys the artifice of the Holy One, blessed be He, and His workmanship.... For these abominations the Spirit of Holiness weeps...." (Zohar, Shemot 3b).

But the prohibition has a much more positive side to it: "A Jew is governed by such reverence for life that he trembles lest he tamper unmindfully with the greatest of all divine gifts, the bestowal or withholding of which is the prerogative of God.... In the unborn child lies the mystery and enigma of existence. Confronted by the miracle of life itself, man can only draw back in silence before the wonder of the Lord" (Jr. Orth. *Jewish Thought*, Vol. 10, No. 2. 1968).

Thus respect for life was seen not to be bound up with one culture, or race, or creed, or lack of belief. It was a matter for the whole human family.

Turning to the now 200-year-old Declaration of Independence, which indeed set out in clear terms for the first time what is commonly known as "the American proposition," the covenant under which men from every nation under heaven would gather to form a new republic and society, it was deemed self-evident and, in that sense, taken for granted, that man was endowed with certain inalienable rights that come from his Creator, and that among these rights—note that the list was not taxative—were the right to life, to liberty and to the pursuit of happiness. Human life and human nature were considered sacred and basic to liberty and justice in a land dedicated to the proposition that all men are created equal.

As in the case of some Talmudic law, so the USA in its first century did not recognize the black slaves as full human beings. The principle was beautifully enunciated but the application of it constituted an egregious and unjust denial of all that the Declaration itself stood for: "All men are created equal." A consensus on such basics should be possible in a state and in society.

At the end of World War II, the Nuremberg trials of the Nazi war criminals were based upon the same principles. Robert Jackson, Attorney General of the United States, drew up, as chief architect, the indictment against the war criminals. He specifically underscored four items: abortion, experimentation on human beings, genocide and euthanasia. In Article Four he asked a basic rhetorical question: "Does it take these men by surprise that murder is considered a crime?" Jackson outlined the history, the laws, the customs, the culture of civilized countries around the world and down through the centuries. He concluded that all nations declare these men were criminals; but he added that in the final analysis these men were human beings, gifted with reason, and therefore responsible, and that they should be not only brought to justice but executed for their crimes precisely because their heinous crimes were against human nature, contrary to humanity itself.

Other codes move along the same lines. The Helsinki Declaration on Human Rights emphasized the sanctity of life in experimentation on human beings; doctors or experimenters must at all times be the protectors of life and health of the person upon whom they are experimenting. The Declaration of Rights of the United Nations insists that all men recognize the inherent dignity and equal inalienable right of all members of the human family.

Perhaps it was all summed up so succinctly by the Latin poet when he said, "Homo sum et nil humani alienum a me puto." "I am a human being, and nothing human do I consider alien from myself."

There is a law of nations, a law of human nature that applies to all in its basic thrust and fundamental rationale. The matter is not one of narrow, sectarian, denominational self-interest but rather is so basic, so deep, so fundamental that it transcends all partisan differences. The value of life is a matter for all human beings.

In America as in all nations, people must reassess their moral and ethical positions as their countries move into the new world, a radically different age in every dimension.

Man will never cease to expand his knowledge and increase his purview of the processes of nature and life itself. Let it be clearly affirmed that science and technology must not be stopped, or unreasonably curtailed, precisely because they promise so much for the benefit of future generations.

But values are not generated by science. Similarly, values as defined by theologians and philosophers are not born in a vacuum, without reference to the real world. Thus, the effort to formulate and to delineate the directions of man in this new age have to be interdisciplinary and cooperative in the face of what threatens man and mankind in the years to come.

The call comes then for a moral discourse.

Something of such a discourse took place in 1975 at the Department of Health, Education and Welfare in Washington, D.C.; a blue-ribbon committee drew up rules and regulations for experimentation on human fetuses. Similarly, the scientific communities in both the United States and England, for the first time in their history, voluntarily supported a moratorium on development of recombinant DNA and the threat of genetic transplants. These discourses were undertaken precisely out of moral considerations and human welfare.

Is it not possible, then, that there can be a new synthesis, a new consensus, perhaps, on such a basic proposition as: "Human life ought not to be taken or endangered except when there is a clear and persuasive argument that other claims are ethically prior" (J. Gustafson) or another basic proposition, "Human beings have a dignity and worth which must always be respected, never suppressed or functionally subordinated to any non-personal reality" (J. C. Murray)?

America (and other nations as well) needs a new sense of moral direction and appreciation of the moral dimensions of the new scientific and technological age in which it finds itself. There is a breakdown in American society, a distrust of all institutions, political, scientific, educational, economic, military and religious. Without a public philosophy which will bring America truly into the new scientific age and era on a moral and just basis, dedicated to the American proposition as fashioned in the Declaration of Independence and the Bill of Rights, America is threatened with a realization, in fact, of the "brave new world" within our borders or a destruction of our civilization as we know it. Without a public philosophy which believes that the moral history of a nation is more important than its scientific or military history, no nation can provide liberty and justice for all.

The words of Thomas Jefferson, enshrined in marble at his monument in Washington, D.C., put the matter this way: "Can the liberties of a nation be thought secure when we have removed their only firm basis, a conviction in the minds of the people that these liberties are the gift of God? That they are not to be violated but with His wrath? I tremble for my country when I reflect that God is just; that His justice cannot sleep forever."

Such a public philosophy lies directly and in large measure in the hands not only of experts in all fields of knowledge but of the general public as well. The future of the human race depends upon both and the value they place on human life will be normative!

# CHAPTER TEN

## THE CHURCH AND SCIENCE—1984?

"The Church in no way forbids that each branch of learning have its own principles and methods but, having recognized this freedom, she watches that they do not fall into error by opposing divine doctrine or overstepping their own bounds to usurp the field of faith."

Vatican I
April 24, 1870

"We cannot but deplore certain habits of mind, sometimes found too often among Christians, which do not sufficiently attend to the rightful independence of science."

Vatican II, *Gaudium et Spes*, no. 36

Would it be too much to assume that Pope John Paul II has officially and publicly, if not implicitly, recognized that Huxley's *Brave New World*, and Orwell's *1984* have already arrived some years ahead of schedule? It seems not.

The setting was the Sala Regia (The Royal Hall) of the Vatican apartments; the audience: scientists and ecclesiastics as well as others of the Pontifical Academy of Sciences; the occasion in honor of the 100th birthday of Albert Einstein; the subject "The Deep Harmony Which Unites the Truths of Science and the Truths of Faith"; and the date, November 26, 1979.

Harkening back to Pope Paul VI, who noted that the moral history of a nation takes precedence over its military, economic, or sociological history, His Holiness boldly asserted that the Catholic Church must be both a faithful collaborator and prophetic leader in the circumstances of this age and era. The problems posed for mankind by the phenomenal advances and extraordinary progress of science and technology he perceived to be both practical and urgent.

The Church, he went on, must live and work in harmony with science, nay, with scientists. Albert Einstein deserves a tribute of praise and gratitude because he "made eminent contributions to the progress of science, that is, to the knowledge of truth present in the mystery of the universe." But there is, of course, science and science.

The Church supports the pure research of fundamental science, and of applied science as well, noting in the latter case that, in a special way, "applied science must be united with conscience" lest the human race become victim of the creation of its own hands.

Pure or fundamental sciences, such as physics, chemistry, astronomy, mathematics, must be free and untrammeled, liberated from political domination, international slavery, economic forces, or "intellectual colonialism." They must be faithful to truth and to the Supreme Truth—God. Applied sciences and technology and the so-called human sciences and disciplines which touch peoples' lives intimately, such as psychology, biology, economics, anthropology, and medicine, promise both great benefits and horrendous mischief. They stand as potential for the enhancement of human dignity and freedom in the service of the people of the world, both present and future; and as well for utter devastation and wanton destruction.

Pope John Paul stressed the primacy of moral principle over technological achievement, of persons over things, of the spiritual over the material. Moreover, the Church supports and respects the autonomy of sciences, "for just as religion demands religious freedom, so rightly, science claims freedom of research."

A troika is called for: science, technology and conscience, precisely because "mankind is menaced by what mankind makes"; because the human race can self-destruct.

The locale in the Vatican and the scene itself were significant because they told of a certain curious irony, a historical retribution. The Holy Father, in a marvelous *tour de force*, not only paid tribute to Albert Einstein, the great physicist, but, in the next breath, to Galileo Galilei, a pioneer physicist and astronomer. "Galileo suffered much here—we will not hide the fact—on the part of men and the structures of the Church." His Holiness went further than mere tribute.

He invited theologians, scholars, and historians to collaborate "to examine the case of Galileo in order to open the gates of future collaboration between religion and science, and stop the conflict that has been prolonged down through the centuries."

If Athens had its Socrates; Rome its Coriolanus; France its Dreyfuss, the Church surely has had its Galileo. For three centuries he and his case have become the exemplary symbol of the Church opposed to science, the litmus test of true devotion to the autonomy of science. Great scientists such as Copernicus, Mendel, and Pasteur were deemed worthy of entry into the pantheon of science in spite of, not because of, their Catholic faith.

Illustrations of the point abound. In January, 1918, in the *Harvard Review,* Richard Wilson Boynton mentioned Gàlileo's famous retort to the theologians that, despite his own recantation, the earth really does move around the sun.

" 'After all, it does move'—this is the challenge that he seems to hurl in the name of modern scholarship at the sealed doors of the Vatican.... (Galileo) was silenced, but that settles nothing. The world goes its way, and an institution—even if it be as ancient and august as the Roman Catholic Church— which refuses to move with it, is left behind."

But Boynton concluded with a very perceptive observation: "However, the old Church is wiser than any pope or single generation of her doctors."

Addressing this question, Cardinal Newman wrote: "Does not the condemnation of Galileo prove the implacable opposition of the Church to scientific progress and enlightenment?" *(Apologia* C.V.) Newman answered in the negative, that the case was the exception that proved the rule. But, no straw man, this Galileo!

Vatican II at least *in petto* somewhat vindicated Galileo, who is referred to in a footnote. But Pope John Paul accepted the historical incubus head-on: where the Church and its theologians were wrong, let's say so; and where Galileo was wrong—a thought not always adverted to—let's say so, too.

After all it was Galileo who wrote that "Holy Scripture and nature proceed equally from divine Word, the former dictated, as it were, by the Holy Spirit, the latter as a very faithful executor of God's orders," and, "all that has been discovered and observed in the last few days thanks to the 'telescope' that I have invented (has been accomplished) after having been enlightened by divine grace."

The Pope's address came as no surprise. A few weeks previously at the Congress of the College of Cardinals, fully one-third of the sessions was devoted to the Church and culture. The media preferred to emphasize the other two topics, namely, the Roman Curia, and the financial situation of the Holy See.

Cardinal Garonne presented the Vatican position paper which stressed that the Church within the limits of her means and in accordance with her mission must be interested in science and research. Moreover, the Church must be in permanent contact "with a mutual exchange of first-hand information" about the moral dimensions of scientific and technological discoveries.

The cardinals of the world were requested to send their comments back to the Holy Father "within three months." Pope John Paul sealed the matter with the pledge (in the November 26th address): "I give all my support to this task which will be able to honor the truth of faith and of science, and open the door to future collaboration."

So much for good intentions! But what of the Church and the culture in which it lives?

The 20th century man and woman have tended to look to science and technology as the chief problem-solvers, as the modern savior, even as "miracle worker." There are miracle drugs, instant communications on a world-wide scale, and dazzling events like men walking on the moon, and feats which border on the preternatural. This faith, held by many, if not most, in all cultures of the East as well as the West, that science will somehow see mankind through its troubles, is adhered to tenaciously, even in the face of the menace of atomic destruction and mutual holocaust.

The scientist Ralph Lapp has written: "No one—not even the most brilliant scientist alive today—really knows where science is taking us. We are aboard a train which is gathering speed, racing down a track on which there are an unknown number of switches leading to unknown destinations. No single scientist is in the engine cab and there may be demons at the switch. Most of society is in the caboose looking backward" *(Fut. Shock,* p. 382).

Alvin Toffler (ibid., p. 386) concludes that "technological questions can no longer be answered in technological terms alone. They are political questions...and we cannot casually delegate responsibility for such decisions to businessmen, scientists, engineers, or administrators who are unaware of the profound consequences of their own actions."

But these consequences to the human race cannot be calculated without moral values. Hence there must enter the realm of religion, of theology, morality, and ethics; hence there must enter the agents of these disciplines—not the least of whom is the Catholic Church.

Future statements of the Church at whatever level should not be timid or diffident about stating that science does not and indeed cannot generate even its own values. In spite of, or perhaps precisely because of "l'affaire Galileo," scientists, theologians and philosophers alike should not hesitate to insist on the limitations of both science and theology, and even more of technology and its relationship to the human race in terms of human freedom and personal dignity.

Herein lies a *pastoral* responsibility because so many people have been led to hold a faith in science that accepts blindly at times a value system based on invalid premises. The Church must not be afraid to say so. Nor must the Church hesitate to apply the direct scrutiny of dogmatic and moral theologians to science, who in turn must keep *au courrant* with the new data. Theologians and philosophers must act as simultaneously with scientists as possible, not simply re-act. The Church can easily fall out-of-date in the face of the rapid progress of science.

Abortion is a primary issue but there are many more: test-tube babies with *in vitro* fertilization; Nobel prize winners' sperm bank with its pre-fabrication of man so consonant with the concept of "superman" and the horrors of holocaust and boat-people; newer drugs for contraception; life-support systems and euthanasia; natural family planning; psycho-surgery; the splicing of genes under the recombinant DNA techniques; the potential for weal or woe of computers and data banks; energy, atomic weaponry and atomic wastes—these and dozens of other major problems call for early discovery, early exposure, simultaneous translation on the part of scientists and theologians, and a clean-cut pastoral response on the part of the Church.

Robert Brungs, S.J., Consultant to the Secretariat for Non-Believers in Rome, has pointed out that the Vatican II document *Gaudium et Spes,* "The Church in the Modern World," was published twelve years *after* the discovery of the structure of DNA, a discovery potentially as significant as the splitting of the atom, and seven years *after* the production through technology of the new contraceptive pills with devastating results. Yet Vatican II did not really address these matters except in perhaps a most general way. Vatican II, however, did offer support for scientists.

Too often it has been assumed in the Church that there is a natural antagonism between the Church and science. The Pope's address on Einstein and Galileo both illustrates the point and suggests a remedy. It has often been assumed that scientists are, *ex professo* at least, agnostics or non-believers, of whom many see the Church as hostile. No doubt there is a correlation, perhaps somewhat high, between science and agnosticism. But there is yet another side.

There are literally thousands of scientists who are genuinely concerned about the moral implications of the work of their hands. The history of the Manhattan Project with its Hiroshima and Nagasaki bombs is a case in point, where scientists expressed their moral reservations to President Harry Truman *prior* to his decision to drop the bombs. Dr. Bernard Nathanson, author of *Aborting America*—he who presided over a mill that has taken over 75,000 lives of the unborn, he who professes atheism—yet has revolted in protest about the moral implications of what is happening in the USA. "I now regret this loss of life" is testimony to his change of mind and conscience as ethics caught up with technology in his experience.

There are Catholic, Christian and other scientists looking for a mandate from the Church to be a leaven in the scientific community. The common dichotomy which so often speaks of the Church *and* the world, of atheism *and* science on the one hand, of science *and* unbelief as though they were synonymous, is most unfortunate and misleading. The Church is *in* the modern world. There are scientists who are Catholic, Protestant, Orthodox, Jewish, Muslim, Buddhist, Hindu—the categories cut through all lines. The Pope put it this way: "...believing and non-believing scientists collaborate, concurring in the search for scientific truth and in respect for belief of others...(endeavoring) to decipher the palimpsest of nature...." But one thing is certain: The American Church must take the lead, precisely because the major portion of research both by quality and quantity is being done within the USA. The Church of the USA by its very position must assume a leadership role in the interests not only of its own country but of the Church universal and mankind universal as well.

The Church was described at Vatican II first as "a sacrament" to the world, thus a visible sign of inward grace to people, all of them. The new dimensions of the world of science and technology, dimensions which are not simply changes in degree but rather in kind, not simply quantity but quality, are in the providence of God and the purview of the human race.

Believers are mandated, by reason of the Incarnation, to know, respect and love all of creation. Christ became truly part of physical creation, entering its history forever. The entire cosmos from its smallest atom to its far edges is a human world, and human beings are the stewards and ministers of this creation. Science and technology are allies of the human race in its pilgrimage back to its Creator.

Science contributes to the human patrimony by yielding an understanding of reality. New discoveries call for a re-working of the philosophical and theological framework in which the human mind lives and has its being. The works of Newton, Darwin, Einstein, the quantum physicists, Watson and Crick of double helix and DNA fame, the space scientists, and many others render a better understanding of the unities of creation. Theirs is not a "forever" framework, even as those of Aristotle, Plato, Aquinas, and Kant were not. But all assisted in the profoundly human search for meaning.

Science, moreover, can enlighten man's understanding of revelation. The virgin birth, transubstantiation, the genetic meaning of masculinity and femininity, the meaning of sexuality, the nature of human life, neural unity and many other questions receive some light from science and add to the understanding and appreciation of what it means to be an *imago Dei*, made to the image and likeness of God.

The *Brave New World* and *1984* have already arrived. Pope John Paul II has taken notice! And his votum to the scientists was one of optimism: "I wish you (scientists) a healthy optimism...which draws its mysterious but real origin from God in whom you have put your faith, or from the unknown God to whom the truth, which is the object of your enlightened researches, is directed."

The Church is challenged to be a "prophetic voice" in the world of science with its firm base in religion and Gospel values, not in the politics, sociology, or psychology of science and technology. Many moral questions can be solved in terms of natural law and natural ethics, but there are some that yield only to the revealed word of God: "Christ is our reality."

The Church teaches with authority, but it cannot do so in a vacuum. Both scientists and theologians play an essential role and the Church needs them together in an unambiguous relationship and collaborative contact.

Science has a way of mesmerizing both the press and the public. "Sensational discoveries" exaggerated in the media constitute a pastoral as well as a science problem. Scientists are equipped to assess the true potential of popularly ballyhooed discoveries, to distinguish fantasy from hard fact. The Church can be too quick to re-act or too dilatory.

St. Gregory Nazianzen (DeVrd. Theol. No. 22) in the fifth century perceived that "to form conclusions too quickly is unscientific; to avoid conclusions is atheistic." If man avoids the conclusions of science, he really denies himself, his place in the cosmos, and the Holy Spirit revealing Himself to the world in the discovery of the nature and secrets of creation. In a word, St. Gregory says, man denies his Creator.

The protection of human values in the new world, the counteraction of the disillusionment of people, of the "ghetto" Catholics and others alienated from science; the protection of the Church against sliding downhill to irrelevancy in modern society by reason of isolation from modern research; the welcoming of the advances of sciences while at the same time refusing to baptize every new change as it occurs; the fostering of the proposition that truth is one and cannot stand in contradiction to itself; the rejection of modernism which would reduce the Church to a mere human face denying its divine origins and nature; the equal rejection of integralism which would make the Church because of its other-worldliness an out-of-the-world community divorced from God's creation, divorced from the Incarnation and history—these are all part and parcel of the prophetic function of the Church, its people, its experts.

The Church's prophetic role is to save the world, not conquer it. The Roman breviary offers a special prayer:

"O God, whose will it is that man should seek out the secrets of nature and so rule the earth, grant that all branches of science and art may serve your glory and promote the well-being of man."

The Church's stance towards science, then, is a positive and supportive one; its prophetic voice must be heard in the "brave new world."

# APPENDICES

*Appendix One*

# DEEP HARMONY WHICH UNITES THE TRUTHS OF SCIENCE WITH THE TRUTHS OF FAITH

*On November 10, 1979, the Pontifical Academy of Sciences commemorated the centenary of the birth of Albert Einstein, with an Academic Session, presided over by the Holy Father in the Sala Regia.*
*John Paul II delivered the following address.*

Venerable Brothers,
Your Excellency,
Ladies and Gentlemen,

1. I thank you heartily, Mr. President, for the warm and fervent words you addressed to me at the beginning of your discourse. And I rejoice also with Your Excellency, as with Mr. Dirac and Mr. Weisskopf, both illustrious members of the Pontifical Academy of Sciences, in this solemn commemoration of the centenary of the birth of Albert Einstein.

The Apostolic See also wishes to pay to Albert Einstein the tribute due to him for the eminent contribution he made to the progress of science, that is, to knowledge of the truth present in the mystery of the universe.

I feel in full solidarity with my Predecessor Pius XI and with those who succeeded him in Peter's See, in calling upon members of the Pontifical Academy of Sciences, and all scientists with them, to bring about "the progress of sciences more and more nobly and intensely, without asking anything else of them; and that because the mission of serving truth, with which we charge them, consists in this excellent intention and in this noble labor..." (Motu Proprio *In multis solaciis* of October 28, 1936, on the Pontifical Academy of Sciences: *AAS* 28, 1936, p. 424).

## To Know Truth

2. The search for truth is the task of basic science. The researcher who moves on this first versant of science feels all the fascination of St. Augustine's words: *"Intellectum valde ama" (Epist.* 120, 3, 13; PL 33, 459), "He loves intelligence" and the function that is characteristic of it, to know truth. Pure science is a good which every people must be able to cultivate in full freedom from all forms of international slavery or intellectual colonialism.

Basic research must be free with regard to the political and economic authorities, which must cooperate in its development without hampering it in its creativity or harnessing it to serve their own purposes. Like any other truth, scientific truth is, in fact, answerable only to itself and to the supreme Truth, God, the Creator of man and of all things.

## United with Conscience

3. On its second versant, science turns to practical applications, which find their full development in the various technologies. In the phase of its concrete achievements, science is necessary to mankind to satisfy the rightful requirements of life, and to overcome the different ills that threaten it. There is no doubt that applied science has rendered and will continue to render immense services to man, provided it is inspired by love, regulated by wisdom, and accompanied by the courage that defends it against the undue interference of all tyrannical powers. Applied science must be united with conscience, so that, in the trinomial, science-technology-conscience, it is the cause of man's real good that is served.

## The Church Aids Science

4. Unfortunately, as I had occasion to say in my Encyclical *Redemptor hominis*, "The man of today seems ever to be

under threat from what he produces.... This seems to make up the main chapter of the drama of present-day human existence" (no. 15). Man must emerge victorious from this drama which threatens to degenerate into a tragedy, and he must find again his true kingship over the world and his full dominion over the things he produces. At the present time, as I wrote in the same encyclical, "The essential meaning of this 'kingship' and 'dominion' of man over the visible world, which the Creator Himself gave man for his task, consists in the priority of ethics over technology, in the primacy of the person over things, and in the superiority of spirit over matter" (no. 16).

This threefold superiority is maintained to the extent to which the sense of the transcendence of man over the world, and of God over man, is preserved. Exercising her mission of guardian and advocate of both transcendences, the Church considers she is helping science to keep its ideal purity on the versant of basic research, and to carry out its service of man on the versant of its practical applications.

## Religion and Science

5. The Church willingly recognizes, moreover, that she has benefited from science. What the Council said about certain aspects of modern culture must be attributed to it, among others: "As regards religion there is a completely new atmosphere that conditions its practice. On the one hand people are taking a hard look at all magical world-views and prevailing superstitions and demanding a more personal and active commitment of faith, so that not a few have achieved a lively sense of the divine" (Gaudium et spes, no. 7).

The collaboration between religion and modern science is to the advantage of both, without violating their respective autonomy in any way. Just as religion demands religious freedom, so science rightly claims freedom of research. The Second Vatican Council, after reaffirming, with the First Vatican Council, the rightful freedom of the arts and of human disciplines in the field of their own principles and their own method, solemnly recognizes "the legitimate autonomy of culture and especially of the sciences" (*Gaudium et spes*, no. 59). On the occasion of this solemn commemoration of Einstein, I would like to confirm again the declarations of the Council on the autonomy of science in its function of research on the truth inscribed in creation by the finger of God. The Church, filled with admiration for the genius of the great scientist in whom the imprint of the creative Spirit is revealed, without intervening in any way with a judgment which it does not fall upon her to pass on the doctrine concerning the great systems of the universe, proposes the latter, however, to the reflection of theologians to discover the harmony existing between scientific truth and revealed truth.

## The Galileo Case

6. Mr. President! You said, very rightly, in your address, that Galileo and Einstein characterized an era. The greatness of Galileo is known to everyone, like that of Einstein; but unlike the latter, whom we are honoring today before the College of Cardinals in the apostolic palace, the former had to suffer a great deal—we cannot conceal the fact—at the hands of men and organisms of the Church. The Vatican Council recognized and deplored certain unwarranted interventions: "We cannot but deplore"—it is written in number 36 of the Conciliar Constitution *Gaudium et spes*—"certain attitudes (not unknown among Christians) deriving from a shortsighted view of the rightful autonomy of science; they have occasioned conflict and controversy and have misled many into thinking that faith and science are opposed." The reference to Galileo is clearly expressed in the note to this text, which cites the volume *Vita e opere di Galileo Galilei,* by Mons. Pio Paschini, published by the Pontifical Academy of Sciences.

To go beyond this stand taken by the Council, I hope that theologians, scholars and historians, animated by a spirit of sincere collaboration, will study the Galileo case more deeply and, in loyal recognition of wrongs from whatever side they come, will dispel the mistrust that still opposes, in many minds, a fruitful concord between science and faith, between the Church and the world. I give all my support to this task, which will be able to honor the truth of faith and of science and open the door to future collaboration.

## Set in True Light

7. Allow me, gentlemen, to submit to your attention and your reflection some points that seem to me important to set again in its true light the Galileo affair. For in this affair the agreements between religion and science are more numerous and above all more important than the incomprehensions which led to the bitter and painful conflict that continued in the course of the following centuries.

He who is rightly called the founder of modern physics declared explicitly that the two truths, of faith and of science, can never contradict each other, "Holy Scripture and nature proceeding equally from the divine Word, the former dictated, as it were, by the Holy Spirit, the latter as a very faithful executor of God's orders," as he wrote in his letter to Father Benedetto Castelli on December 21, 1613 (National Edition of the Works of Galileo, vol. V, pp. 282-285). The Second Vatican Council does not express itself otherwise: it even takes up again similar expressions when it teaches: "Methodical research in all branches of knowledge, provided it is carried out in a truly scientific manner and does not override moral laws, can never conflict with the faith, because the things of the world and the things of faith derive from the same God" (Gaudium et spes, no. 36).

## Creator Ever Present

Galileo feels in his scientific research the presence of the Creator, who stimulates him, inspires and helps his intuitions, acting in the deepest recesses of his spirit. In connection with the invention of the telescope, he writes at the beginning of Sidereus Nuncius, recalling some of his astronomical discoveries: "Quae omnia ope Perspicilli a me excogitati divina prius illuminante gratia, paucis abhinc diebus reperta, atque observata fuerunt" (Sidereus Nuncius, Venetiis, apud

Thomas Baglionum, MDCX, fol. 4). "All that has been discovered and observed in the last few days thanks to the 'telescope' that I have invented, after having been enlightened by divine grace."

Galileo's confession of divine illumination in the mind of the scientist finds an echo in the text already quoted of the Conciliar Constitution on the Church in the Modern World: "The humble and persevering investigator of the secrets of nature is being led, as it were, by the hand of God in spite of himself" (loc. cit.).

The humility which the conciliar text stresses is a virtue of the spirit necessary for scientific research as well as for adherence to faith. Humility creates a climate favorable to the dialogue between the believer and the scientist; it calls for the illumination of God, already known or still unknown, but loved in both cases by him who humbly seeks the truth.

## Galileo's Norms

8. Galileo formulated important norms of an epistemological character, which are indispensable to reconcile Holy Scripture and science. In his letter to the grand duchess mother of Tuscany, Christine of Lorraine, he reaffirms the truth of the Scriptures: "Holy Scripture can never lie, provided, however, that its real meaning is understood. The latter—I do not think it can be denied—is often hidden and very different from what the mere sense of the words seems to indicate" (National Edition of the Works of Galileo, vol. V, p. 315). Galileo introduces the principle of an interpretation of the sacred books which goes beyond the literal meaning but is in conformity with the intention and the type of exposition characteristic of them. It is necessary, as he affirms, that "the wise men who expound it should show its real meaning."

The ecclesiastical Magisterium admits the plurality of the rules for the interpretation of Holy Scripture. It teaches expressly in fact, with Pius XII's encyclical, *Divino afflante*

*Spiritu,* the presence of different literary styles in the sacred books and therefore the necessity of interpretations in conformity with the character of each of them.

The various agreements that I have mentioned do not in themselves solve all the problems of the Galileo affair, but they contribute to creating a starting point favorable to their honorable solution, a state of mind propitious to the honest and loyal solution of old oppositions.

The existence of this Pontifical Academy of Sciences, with which Galileo was associated in a certain way through the old institution which preceded the present one to which eminent scientists belong today, is a visible sign which manifests, without any form of racial or religious discrimination, the deep harmony that can exist between the truths of science and the truths of faith.

## Pontifical Academy

9. In addition to the foundation of your Pontifical Academy by Pius XI, my predecessor John XXIII wished the Church to continue to promote scientific progress and to reward it, by establishing the Pius XI Medal. In conformity with the choice made by the Council of the Academy, I am happy to confer this high distinction on a young researcher, Dr. Antonio Paes de Carvalho, whose basic research works have made an important contribution to the progress of science and the good of mankind.

## The Church and Scientific Progress

10. Mr. President and members of the Academy, before the Lords Cardinals present here, the Diplomatic Corps accredited to the Holy See, the illustrious scientists and all the personalities attending this academic session, I would like to declare that the universal Church, the Church of Rome united with all those in the world, attaches great importance to the function of the Pontifical Academy of Sciences.

The title "Pontifical" attributed to this Academy signifies, as you know, the interest and support of the Church. These are manifested in very different forms, of course, from those of ancient patronage, but they are no less deep and effective. As the distinguished President of your Academy, the late Mons. Lemaître, wrote: "Does the Church need science? Certainly not, the cross and the Gospel are sufficient for her. But nothing human is alien to the Christian. How could the Church have failed to take an interest in the most noble of the strictly human occupations: the search for truth?" (O. Godart—M. Heller, *Les relations entre la science et la foi chez Georges Lemaître. Pontificia Academia Scientiarum, Commentarii,* vol. III, no. 21, p. 7)

In this Academy which is yours and mine, believing and non-believing scientists collaborate, concurring in the search for scientific truth and in respect for the beliefs of others. Allow me to quote here again a luminous passage by Mons. Lemaître: "Both of them (the believing scientist and the non-believing scientist) endeavor to decipher the palimpsest of nature, in which the traces of the various stages of the long evolution of the world are overlaid on one another and confused. The believer has perhaps the advantage of knowing that the enigma has a solution, that the underlying writing is, when all is said and done, the work of an intelligent being, therefore that the problem raised by nature had been raised in order to be solved, and that its difficulty is doubtless proportionate to the present or future capacity of mankind. That will not give him, perhaps, new resources in his investigation, but it will contribute to maintaining in him a healthy optimism without which a sustained effort cannot be kept up for long" (o.c., p. 11).

I wish you all this healthy optimism of which Mons. Lemaître speaks, an optimism which draws its mysterious but real origin from God, in whom you have put your faith, or from the unknown God to whom the truth, which is the object of your enlightened researches, is directed.

May the science that you profess, members of the Academy and scientists, in the field of pure research as in that of applied research, help mankind, with the support of religion and in agreement with it, to find again the way to hope and to reach the last aim of peace and faith!

*Appendix Two*

# STUDY THE WORLD TO KNOW MAN

*On Friday, September 28, 1979, the Holy Father received in audience participants in the conference on "The problem of the cosmos," promoted by the Institute of the Italian Encyclopaedia to honor Albert Einstein on the first centenary of his birth.*
*John Paul II addressed the group (in part).*

*The problem of the cosmos!* A subject rich in immense fascination for present-day man, as for the man of the past; for the man of always.

## Science of Totality

What a stupendous science is yours, which, in the field of researches on nature, takes its place in a certain way at the summit of all the others, since its inquiry does not refer to a particular field of nature itself and its phenomena, but with a magnificent drive, which exalts and ennobles man's mind, even tries to embrace the immensity of the universe, to penetrate its structure and follow its evolution. Cosmology, a science of the totality of what exists as experimentally observable being, is therefore endowed with a special epistemological status of its own, which sets it more than any other, perhaps, at the borders with philosophy and with religion, since the science of totality leads spontaneously to the question about totality itself, a question which does not find its answers within this totality.

## Highway to Wonder

It is with deep emotion that I speak to you today, students of such a vast science, which unfolds before you the whole of creation. Your science is for man a highway to wonder. The contemplation of the firmament has always been for man a source of absolute amazement, from the most ancient times; but today you guide us, men of the 20th century, along the ways of a new wonder. They are ways that pass through the laborious and patient advance of reason, which has studied nature with wisdom and constancy, with an austere discipline which, in a certain way, has set aside delight in contemplation of the beauty of the sky in order to sound its abysses more and more deeply and systematically.

More and more powerful and ingenious instruments—telescopes, radiotelescopes, space probes—have made it possible to reveal to our astonished minds and eyes objects and phenomena that our imagination would never have dared to conceive—star-clusters, galaxies and groups of galaxies, quasars and pulsars.... They have expanded the frontiers of our knowledge to distances of milliards of light years; they have made it possible for us to go back in time to the most remote past, almost to the origins of that process of expansion of the universe which is one of the most extraordinary and unexpected discoveries of our time.

## "Gratuitous" Science

So scientific reason, after a long journey, makes us discover things again with new wonder. It induces us to raise again with renewed intensity some of the great questions of the man of always: Where do we come from? Where are we going? It leads us to pit ourselves once more against the frontiers of mystery, that mystery of which Einstein said that it is "the fundamental feeling, which is at the side of the cradle of true art and of true science" and, we add, of true metaphysics and true religion.

But I appreciate your science particularly also for another reason. Unlike so many other sciences of nature, which are cultivated and developed with particular solicitude today because they put in man's hands the power to change the world in which he lives, your science is, in a certain sense, a "gratuitous" science. It does not give man power to construct or to destroy, but it satisfies the pure desire, the deep ideal of knowing. And this, in a world strongly tempted by utilitarianism and thirst for command, is a value to bear witness to and to guard. I acknowledge that to you.

But, actually, to get to know the world is not a gratuitous or useless thing; on the contrary, it is supremely necessary in order to know who man is. Not for nothing has the view of the cosmos in different periods and different cultures always been closely connected with, and had a strong influence on, the view that the cultures themselves had of man. Now, if knowledge of the boundless dimensions of the cosmos has cancelled the illusion that our planet or our solar system is the physical center of the universe, not for this reason has man been diminished in his dignity. On the contrary, the adventure of science has made us discover and experience with new vividness the immensity and transcendence of man's spirit, capable of penetrating the abysses of the universe, of delving into its laws, of tracing its history, rising to a level incomparably higher than the other creatures that surround him.

## Mystery of Man

So the words of the ancient psalmist spring spontaneously again to the lips of the twentieth century believer:

"O Lord, our Lord,...
When I look at your heavens, the work of your fingers,
   the moon and the stars which you have established;
what is man that you are mindful of him,
   and the son of man that you care for him?
Yet you have made him little less than the angels..."
   (Ps. 8:2; 4-5; 6a).

As already before the sublimity of creation, so also before man, searching the universe and its laws, our spirit starts with amazement and wonder, since here, too, it touches the mystery.

Is it not a question, fundamentally, of one great mystery: the One that is the root of all things, of the cosmos and its origin, as well as of man who is capable of studying it and understanding it? If the universe is, as it were, an immense word which, though with difficulty and slowly, can at last be deciphered and understood, who is it who says this word to man? The voice and the thought of the believer feel in a tremble after you have led him along the ways and into the depths of immensity, and yet I, a witness of the Faith at the threshold of the third millennium, utter once more with fear and joy the blessed name: God, Creator of heaven and earth, whose love is revealed to us in Christ the Lord.

With these sentiments, I encourage you all to continue your austere studies, while I invoke on you, on your scientific labors, and on your dear ones, the riches of the gifts of the *Pantocrator*, the Lord of heaven and of earth.

*Appendix Three*

# MEETING OF SCIENCE AND FAITH AS MANIFESTATION OF TRUTH

*On April 2, 1981, the Holy Father received the Cardinals and Bishops participating in the plenary assembly of the Secretariat for Non-Believers. The work of the assembly, which lasted from March 31 to April 3, was dedicated to the subject "Science and non-belief." John Paul II delivered the following address.*

Your Eminences,
Dear brothers in the episcopate,
Dear friends,

1. It is a joy for me to meet this morning, for the first time, the participants in the plenary assembly of the Secretariat for Non-Believers, with its new Pro-President and its new members. It is a question, in fact, of developing the stimulus already given by Pope Paul VI with dear Cardinal Franz König and the late Father Vincenzo Miano.

The subject you are now studying, "Science and non-belief," is of vital importance, and the Holy See has long desired to promote a thorough study of it. It is part of the purpose of your Secretariat, which has received as its task both the study of atheism and dialogue with non-believers. It is quite clear to all of you, I know, that it is not a question of a study carried out in an academic way, but of a work of pastoral reflection, which does not exclude either strictness of methods or deep research. Certainly, you cannot dialogue, like the other two Secretariats, with adequate international authorities; your work implies rather relations with the episcopal conferences according to the various socio-cultural situations.

## Science, a Question of Culture

2. From the latter point of view, the subject of your research is a very rich one, if one considers that science is a question of culture, involving important consequences on mentalities, whether we are dealing with natural sciences or human sciences.

To try to understand the totality of reality is a legitimate ambition which honors man and which the believer shares. So there is no opposition at this level, but rather at the level of mentalities, when these are dominated by a scientistic conception according to which the sphere of truth is identified with what can be known and verified experimentally. This positivistic mentality deeply marks modern culture, which is derived from the philosophy that opposes faith on the ideological plane, but not science itself. On the contrary, passionate pursuit of the "hows" calls for an answer to the "whys."

It is the same, in a way, for the human sciences, which are witnessing an increasing development and whose sphere is, moreover, more difficult to define. Do they not succumb to a scientistic pretense far more than they give proof of their real scientific nature, when their promoters tend to present as the ideal model of this type of knowledge a conception reducing man—who is a subject—to an object of studies, researches and experimentations, to the exclusion of the specifically spiritual reality?

3. The development of sciences, through the increase of rationality which it brings, calls finally for an aim of totality which it does not supply: the meaning of meaning. For if it is true that science is a very special form of knowledge, it does not follow that scientific knowledge is the only legitimate form of knowledge. In this radically reductionist perspective, faith would no longer appear except as a naive representation of reality, bound up with a mythological mentality. In a totalizing perspective, on the contrary, it is important to distinguish specific orders clearly, and, far from setting their contents in opposition, to propose their integration in an epiphany of truth.

It is certain that the taking into consideration of the totality of reality is delicate and difficult. Sometimes there is reduction from one order to another; sometimes, on the contrary, it is thought possible to scorn all articulation. A double temptation for believers must be recognized here: rationalism and fideism.

## Science and the Meaning of Life

4. Moreover, more than dealing with an abstract confrontation between scientific unbelief and Christian faith, it is a question of a dialogue among men, in which the dynamics of rationality is not at all opposed to the transcendence of faith in its specific nature, but, in a sense, calls for it. It is in the experience of life that it seems necessary to overcome the interior emptiness resulting from the collapse of meaning, when the totalization of men's activities is set in a closed universe and is no longer assumed in a perspective which transcends them, in a supra-rational plane which, far from being a non-rational or an infra-rational one, is the foundation and the end of rationality.

5. Mention should also be made of a risk inherent in the method of scientific investigation itself. It has its object and its own requirements. But, to the extent that it impregnates the whole of thought, the whole way of considering existence, it can in the sphere of faith lead to loss of the certainty characteristic of faith, where to know is also to love. Thus, this spirit of perpetual search can lead to questioning the essential truths of faith and, without denying them, to suspending judgment and affirmation until one has himself elucidated all reasons for believing and all the aspects of the Christian mystery, as if other discoveries concerning the creed itself could be expected. Certainly, it is necessary, as the Apostle Peter said, always to be capable of accounting for the hope that is in us (cf. 1 Pt. 3:15). And there is real scientific work to be assiduously carried out in theology, exegesis and morality, but relying on a revealed truth, and within a total adherence already given to Jesus Christ and to His Church which does not provisionally put in parentheses the certain

affirmations of the Magisterium. That is for you, naturally, a matter of course; but minds imbued with scientific research may find this a difficulty or an obstacle, for lack of comprehension of the specific and transcendent nature of faith, and they run the risk of remaining on the threshold of faith.

6. It is important to clarify this difficulty, as well as the more radical ones I previously pointed out, and to help our generation to overcome them.

As I said last October 11, in connection with the subject you are studying, "If catechesis is insufficiently informed of the problems of the exact sciences, as well as of human sciences, in their diversity, it may accumulate obstacles in an intelligence, instead of making a way in it to affirmation of God." This is the case when there is a real difference between the present-day image of the world conveyed by the sciences—and above all by the popularization of sciences in the general public—and the traditional expressions of faith, sometimes repeated without caring about real mentalities.

## Science and Faith

7. Finally, how could one forget that scientists themselves recognize that objectivity and rationality, however important they may be, do not meet man's need to understand his destiny? But that is not enough to lead them to recognize a personal and transcendent God. And some turn towards a kind of pantheism with a mystical coloring. Repudiating scientism, that science which has strayed beyond its borders, they equally reject the established Churches, because of the claim for human autonomy and criticisms of a socio-political nature, united with the relativism engendered by the discovery of the various religions and the multiplication of sects.

The meeting between science and faith raises problems which the believer can adequately solve. But the mystery of faith can be lived only in an existential way. And the multiform meeting of atheism, unbelief and indifference calls for the existence of believers with strong convictions and living a Christian experience; in other words, possessing a solid formation, which is not separated from prayer and evangelical witness. Faith is a gift from God, a grace, and, once more, it presupposes love.

## An Important Role To Play

8. Catholic universities, philosophers and theologians, thinkers and writers, for their part, have a considerable role to play: to present a true and credible anthropology through the various cultures, that basic common ground. As I said to UNESCO last June 2: "Man lives a really human life thanks to culture" (no. 6). It is a question of showing how man—and today, man marked by sciences and the scientific spirit—becomes fully man by opening himself to the fullness of the Incarnate Word: "Behold the man."

This shows the importance for the Church of an apostolate of the intelligence. And the Secretariat for Non-Believers owes it to itself to play here an important role of stimulation, deepening, suggestions, and proposals within the Roman Curia and in the service of the local Churches confronted with the challenge of atheism and the tragedy of unbelief, in liaison, of course, with the university competences. In this way it will be able to help many believers to bear witness to the values which constitute their reasons for living, to find the words to share them, and not to be afraid to assert themselves as witnesses of God in the very name of the obstinate search for Truth which, through centuries of scientific research, constitutes the grandeur of mankind.

These reflections do not, of course, exhaust this vast subject. We will come back to it. I hope that you will find in them today an encouragement to continue your work. Keep on opening up a way to the Gospel, keep on building bridges. May the Holy Spirit enlighten you and strengthen you! With my affectionate apostolic blessing.

*Appendix Four*

# MAN'S ENTIRE HUMANITY
# IS EXPRESSED IN CULTURE

*On June 2, 1980, John Paul II met the representatives of UNESCO and delivered the following address.*

Mr. President of the General Conference,
Mr. President of the Executive Council,
Mr. Director General,
Ladies and gentlemen,

1. I wish in the first place to express my very cordial thanks for the invitation that Mr. Amadou Mahtar-M'Bow, Director General of the United Nations Educational, Scientific and Cultural Organization, extended to me several times, even at the first of the visits he has done me the honor of paying me. There are many reasons for which I am happy to be able to accept today this invitation, which I highly appreciated immediately.

For the kind words of welcome they have just addressed to me, I thank Mr. Napoléon Leblanc, President of the General Conference; Mr. Chams Eldine El-Wakil, President of the Executive Council; and Mr. Amadou Mahtar-M'Bow, Director General of the Organization. I also wish to greet all those who are gathered here for the 109th session of UNESCO's Executive Council. I cannot conceal my joy at seeing gathered on this occasion so many delegates from nations all over the world, so many eminent personalities, so many authorities, so many illustrious representatives of the world of culture and science.

Through my intervention, I will try to bring my modest stone to the edifice you are constructing with assiduity and perseverance, ladies and gentlemen, through your reflections and your resolutions in all the fields that are in UNESCO's sphere of competence.

2. Allow me to begin by referring *to the origins of your Organization*. The events that marked the foundation of UNESCO inspire me with joy and gratitude to divine Providence: the signature of its constitution on November 16, 1945; the coming into force of this constitution and the establishment of the Organization on November 4, 1946; the agreement between UNESCO and the United Nations Organization approved by the General Assembly of the U.N. in the same year. Your Organization is, in fact, the work of the nations which, after the end of the terrible second world war, were impelled by what could be called a spontaneous desire for peace, union and reconciliation. These nations looked for the means and the forms of a collaboration capable of establishing this new understanding and of deepening it and ensuring it in a lasting way. So UNESCO came into being, like the United Nations Organization, because the peoples knew that, at the basis of the great enterprises intended to serve peace and the progress of humanity over the whole globe, there was *the necessity of the union of nations,* mutual respect and international cooperation.

3. Prolonging the action, thought and message of my great Predecessor Pope Paul VI, I had the honor of speaking before the United Nations General Assembly, in the month of October last, on the invitation of Mr. Kurt Waldheim, Secretary General of U.N. Shortly afterwards, on November 12, 1979, I was invited by Mr. Edouard Saouma, Director General of the United Nations Food and Agricultural Organization in Rome. On these occasions I had the honor of dealing with questions deeply linked with all the problems connected with man's peaceful future on earth. In fact, all these problems are closely linked. We are in the presence, so to speak, of a vast system of communicating vessels: the problems of culture, science and education do not arise, in the life of nations and in international relations, independently of the other problems of human existence, such as those of peace or hunger. The problems of culture are conditioned by the other dimensions of human existence, just as the latter, in their turn, condition them.

4. All the same, there is—and I stressed it in my address to the U.N., referring to the Universal Declaration of Human Rights—one fundamental dimension, which is capable of shaking to their very foundations the systems that structure mankind as a whole and of freeing human existence, individual and collective, from the threats that weigh on it. This fundamental dimension is man, man in his integrality, man who lives at the same time in the sphere of material values and in that of spiritual values. Respect for the inalienable rights of the human person is at the basis of everything (cf. Address to the U.N., nos. 7 and 13).

Any threat to human rights, whether in the framework of man's spiritual goods or in that of his material goods, does violence to this fundamental dimension. That is why, in my address to FAO, I emphasized that no man, no country and no system in the world can remain indifferent to the "geography of hunger" and the gigantic threats that will ensue if the whole direction of economic policy, and in particular the hierarchy of investments, do not change in an essential and radical way. That is also why, referring to the origins of your Organization, I stress the necessity of mobilizing all forces which direct the spiritual dimension of human existence, and which bear witness to the primacy of the spiritual in man—and of what corresponds to the dignity of his intelligence, his will and his heart—in order not to succumb again to the monstrous alienation of collective evil, which is always ready to use material powers in the exterminating struggle of men against men, of nations against nations.

5. At the origin of UNESCO, as also at the basis of the Universal Declaration of Human Rights, there are, therefore, these first noble impulses of human conscience, intelligence and will. I appeal to this origin, to this beginning, to these premises and to these first principles. It is in their name that I come today to Paris, to the headquarters of your Organization, with an entreaty: that at the end of a stage of over thirty years of your activities, you will unite even more round these ideals and principles on which the beginning was based. It is in their name also that I shall now take the liberty of proposing to you some really fundamental considerations, for it is only by their

light that there shines forth fully the meaning of this institution, which has as its name UNESCO, the United Nations Educational, Scientific and Cultural Organization.

6. *Genus humanum arte et ratione vivit* (cf. St. Thomas, commenting on Aristotle, in *Post. Analyt.*, no. 1). These words of one of the greatest geniuses of Christianity, who was at the same time a fruitful continuer of the thought of antiquity, take us beyond the circle and contemporary meaning of Western culture, whether it is Mediterranean or Atlantic. They have a meaning that applies to humanity as a whole, where the different traditions that constitute its spiritual heritage and the different periods of its culture meet. The essential meaning of culture consists, according to these words of St. Thomas Aquinas, in the fact that it is a characteristic of human life as such. *Man lives a really human life thanks to culture.* Human life is culture in this sense too that, through it, man is distinguished and differentiated from everything that exists elsewhere in the visible world: man cannot do without culture.

Culture is a specific way of man's "existing" and "being." Man always lives according to a culture which is specifically his, and which, in its turn, creates among men a tie which is also specifically theirs, determining the inter-human and social character of human existence. *In the unity* of culture as the specific way of human existence, there is rooted at the same time the *plurality of cultures* in the midst of which man lives. In this plurality, man develops without losing, however, the essential contact with the unity of culture as the fundamental and essential dimension of his existence and his being.

7. Man who, in the visible world, is *the only* ontic *subject of culture*, is also *its only object and its term.* Culture is that through which man, as man, becomes more man, "is" more, has more access to "being." The fundamental distinction between what man is and what he has, between being and having, has its foundation there too. Culture is always in an essential and necessary relationship to what man is, whereas its relationship to what he has, to his "having," is not only secondary, but entirely relative. All man's "having" is impor-

tant for culture, is a factor creative of culture, only to the extent to which man, through his "having," can at the same time "be" more fully as a man, become more fully a man in all the dimensions of his existence, in everything that characterizes his humanity. The experience of the various eras, without excluding the present one, proves that people think of culture and speak about it *in the first place in relation to the nature of man,* then only *in a secondary and indirect way in relation to the world of his products.* That in no way detracts from the fact that we judge the phenomenon of culture on the basis of what man produces, or that we draw from that, at the same time, conclusions about man. Such an approach—a typical way of the "a posteriori" process of knowledge—contains in itself the possibility of going back, in the opposite direction, to ontic-causal dependencies. Man, and only man, is the "protagonist," or "architect" of culture; man, and only man, expresses himself in it and finds his own balance in it.

## The Complete Man the Subject of Culture

8. All of us present here meet *on the ground of culture, the fundamental reality* which unites us and which is at the basis of the establishment and purposes of UNESCO. We thereby meet around man and, in a certain sense, in him, in man. This *man,* who expresses himself and objectivizes himself in and through culture, is *unique, complete* and *indivisible.* He is at once subject and architect of culture. Consequently, he cannot be envisaged solely as the resultant—to give only one example—of the production relations that prevail at a given period. Is this criterion of production relations not at all, then, *a key to the understanding* of man's historicity, to the understanding of his culture and of the multiple forms of his development? Certainly, this criterion is a key, and even a precious key, but it is not the fundamental, constitutive one. Human cultures reflect, there is no doubt, the various systems of production relations; however, it is not such and such a system that is at the origin of culture, but man, man who lives in the system, who accepts it or tries to change it. A culture

without human subjectivity and without human causality is inconceivable; in the cultural field, *man is always the first fact: man is the prime and fundamental fact of culture.*

And he is so, always, in his totality: *in his spiritual and material subjectivity as a complete whole.* If the distinction between spiritual culture and material culture is correct with respect to the character and content of the products in which the culture is manifested, it is necessary to note at the same time that, on the one hand, the works of material culture always show a *"spiritualization of matter"*—a submission of the material element to man's spiritual forces, that is, his intelligence and will—and that, on the other hand, the works of spiritual culture manifest, specifically, a *"materialization"* of *the spirit,* an incarnation of what is spiritual. In cultural works, this double characteristic seems to be equally of prime importance and equally permanent.

Here is, therefore, by way of theoretical conclusion, a sufficient basis to understand culture through the complete man, through the whole reality of his subjectivity. Here is also—in the field of action—a sufficient basis to seek always in culture the complete man, the whole man, in the whole truth of his spiritual and corporeal subjectivity; the basis which is sufficient in order *not to superimpose* on culture—a truly human system, a splendid synthesis of spirit and body—*preconceived divisions and oppositions.* In fact, whether it is a question of an absolutization of matter in the structure of the human subject, or, inversely, of an absolutization of the spirit in this same structure, neither expresses the truth about man nor serves his culture.

9. I would like to stop here at another essential consideration, a reality of a quite different order. We can approach it by noting the fact that the Holy See is represented at UNESCO by its permanent Observer, whose presence is set in the perspective of the very nature of the Apostolic See. This presence is, even more widely, in harmony with the nature and mission of the Catholic Church and, indirectly, with that of the whole of Christianity. I take the opportunity which is offered to me today to express a deep personal conviction. *The presence of the Apostolic See* in your organization—though motivated also

by the specific sovereignty of the Holy See—has its justification above all in *the organic and constitutive link* which exists between *religion* in general and Christianity in particular, on the one hand, and *culture*, on the other hand. This relationship extends to the multiple realities which must be defined as concrete expressions of culture in the different periods of history and all over the world. It will certainly not be an exaggeration to state in particular that, through a multitude of facts, the whole of Europe—from the Atlantic to the Urals—bears witness, in the history of each nation as in that of the whole community, to the link between culture and Christianity.

Recalling this, it is not at all my intention to belittle the heritage of other continents, or the specific character and value of this same heritage which is derived *from the other* sources of religious, humanistic and ethical inspiration. What is more, I wish to pay *the deepest and most sincere tribute* to all the cultures of the human family as a whole, from the most ancient to the contemporary. It is in thinking of all cultures that I wish to say in a loud voice, here in Paris, at the headquarters of UNESCO, with respect and admiration: "Here is man!" I wish to proclaim my admiration before the creative riches of the human spirit, before its incessant efforts to know and strengthen *the identity of man:* this man who is always present in all the particular forms of culture.

10. Speaking, on the contrary, of the *place of the Church* and of the Apostolic See in your Organization, I am thinking not only of all the works of culture in which, in the course of the last two millennia, the man who had accepted Christ and the Gospel expressed himself, or of the institutions of different kinds that came into being from the same inspiration in the fields of education, instruction, charity, social work and in so many others. I am thinking above all, ladies and gentlemen, *of the fundamental link between the Gospel, that is, the message of Christ and the Church, and man in his very humanity.* This link is in fact a creator of culture in its very foundation. To create culture, it is necessary to consider, to its last consequences and entirely, man as a particular and autonomous value, as the subject bearing the transcendency

of the person. Man must *be affirmed for himself,* and not for any other motive or reason: solely for himself! What is more, man must be loved because he is man; love must be claimed for man by reason of the particular dignity he possesses. The whole of the affirmations concerning man belong to the very substance of Christ's message and of the mission of the Church, in spite of all that critics may have declared about this matter, and all that the different movements opposed to religion in general and to Christianity in particular may have done.

In the course of history, we have already been more than once, and we still are, *witnesses of a process of a very significant phenomenon.* Where *religious institutions* have been suppressed, where ideas and works born of religious inspiration, and in particular of Christian inspiration, have been deprived of their citizenship, men find again these same elements *outside institutional ways,* through the confrontation operated, in truth and interior effort, between what constitutes their humanity and what is contained in the Christian message.

Ladies and gentlemen, you will kindly forgive my making this statement. Proposing it, I did not want to offend anyone at all. I beg you to understand that, in the name of what I am, *I could not abstain from giving this testimony.* It also bears within it this truth—which cannot be passed over in silence—on culture, if we seek in it everything that is human, the elements in which man expresses himself or through which he wants to be the subject of his existence. And in so speaking, I wanted at the same time to *manifest* all the more *my gratitude* for the ties that unite UNESCO with the Apostolic See, these ties of which my presence today is intended as a particular expression.

11.  A certain number of fundamental conclusions can be drawn from all that. In fact, the considerations I have just made show clearly that *the primary and essential task of culture* in general, and also of all culture, *is education.* Education consists in fact in enabling man to become more man, to "be" more and not just to "have" more and, consequently, through everything he "has," everything he possesses, to "be" man more fully. For this purpose man must be able to "be more"

not only "with others," but also "for others." Education is of fundamental importance for the formation of inter-human and social relations. Here, too, I touch upon a set of axioms on the basis of which the traditions of Christianity that have sprung from the Gospel meet the educative experience of so many well-disposed and deeply wise men, so numerous in all centuries of history. In our age, too, there is no lack of them, of these *men who reveal themselves as great,* simply through their *humanity which they are able to share* with others, in particular with the young. At the same time, the symptoms of crises of all kinds to which there succumb environments and societies which are among those best-off in other ways—crises which affect above all young generations—vie with each other in bearing witness that the work of man's education *is not carried out only with the help of institutions,* with the help of organized and material means, however excellent they may be. They also show that the most important thing is always man, man and his *moral authority* which comes from the truth of his principles and from the conformity of his actions with these principles.

12. As the world organization most competent in all problems of culture, UNESCO cannot neglect this other question which is absolutely fundamental: what can be done in order that man's education may be carried out *above all in the family?*

What is the state of public morality which will ensure the family, and above all the parents, of the moral authority necessary for this purpose? What type of instruction? What forms of legislation sustain this authority or, on the contrary, weaken it or destroy it? The causes of success and failure in the formation of man by his family always lie both *within* the fundamental creative environment of culture which the family is, and also *at a higher level,* that of the competence of the state and the organs, on which these causes depend. These problems cannot but cause reflection and solicitude in the forum where the qualified representatives of the state meet.

There is no doubt that the first and fundamental cultural fact is the spiritually mature man, that is, a fully educated man, a man capable of educating himself and educating others. Nor is there any doubt that the first and fundamental dimension of culture is healthy morality: *moral culture.*

13. Certainly, there are many particular questions in this field, but experience shows that everything is connected, and that these questions are set in systems that plainly depend upon one another. For example, in the process of education as a whole, and of scholastic education in particular, has there not been *a unilateral shift towards instruction in the narrow sense of the word?* If we consider the proportions assumed by this phenomenon, as well as the systematic increase of instruction which refers solely to what man possesses, is not man himself put more and more in the shade? That leads, then, to a real *alienation of education:* instead of working in favor of what man must "be," it works solely in favor of what man can take advantage of in the field of "having," of "possession." The further stage of this alienation is to accustom man, by depriving him of his own subjectivity, to being the *object of multiple manipulations:* ideological or political manipulations which are carried out through public opinion; those that are operated through monopoly or control, through economic forces or political powers, and the media of social communication; finally, the manipulation which consists of teaching life as a specific manipulation of oneself.

## The Apparent Imperatives of Our Society

These dangers in the field of education seem to threaten above all societies with a more developed technical civilization. These societies are confronted with man's specific *crisis* which consists of *a growing lack of confidence with regard to his own humanity,* to the meaning of the fact of being a man, and to the affirmation and joy derived from it, which are a source of creation. Modern civilization tries to impose on man a series of *apparent imperatives,* which its spokesmen justify by recourse to the principle of development and progress. Thus, for example, instead of respect for life, "the imperative" of getting rid of life and destroying it; instead of love which is the responsible communion of persons, "the imperative" of the maximum sexual enjoyment apart from any sense of responsibility; instead of the primacy of truth in actions, the "primacy" of behavior that is fashionable, of the subjective, and of immediate success.

In all that, there is indirectly expressed a great *systematic renunciation* of the healthy ambition of being a man. Let us be under no illusions: the system constructed on the basis of these false imperatives, these fundamental renunciations, may determine the future of man and the future of culture.

14. If, in the name of the future of culture, it must be proclaimed that man has the right to "be" more, and if for the same reason it is necessary to demand a healthy *primacy of the family* in the overall work of educating man to real humanity, *the law of the nation* must be set along the same line; it, too, must be placed *at the basis of culture and education.*

The nation is, in fact, the great community of men who are united by various ties, but, above all, precisely by culture. The nation exists *"through" culture and "for" culture,* and it is therefore the great educator of men in order that they may "be more" in the community. It is this community which possesses a history that goes beyond the history of the individual and the family. It is also in this community, with respect to which every family educates, that the family begins its work of education with what is the most simple thing, language, thus enabling man who is at the very beginning to learn to speak in order to become a member of the community of his family and of his nation.

In all that I am now proclaiming, which I will develop still further, my words express a particular experience, *a particular testimony* in its kind. I am the son of a nation which has lived the greatest experiences of history, which its neighbors have condemned to death several times, but which has survived and remained itself. It has kept its identity, and it has kept, in spite of partitions and foreign occupations, its national sovereignty, not by relying on the resources of physical power, but solely by relying on its culture. This culture turned out in the circumstances to be more powerful than all other forces.

What I say here concerning the right of the nation to the foundation of its culture and its future is not, therefore, the echo of any "nationalism," but it is always a question of a stable element of human experience and of the *humanistic perspective of man's development.* There exists a fundamental sovereignty of society which is manifested in the culture of the nation. It is a question of the sovereignty through which, at the same time, man is supremely sovereign. When I express myself in this way, I am also thinking, with deep interior emotion, of the cultures of so many ancient peoples which did not give way when confronted with the civilizations of the invaders: and they still remain for man the source of his "being" as a man in the interior truth of his humanity. I am also thinking with admiration of the cultures of new societies, those that are awakening to life in the community of their own nation—just as my nation awakened to life ten centuries ago—and that are struggling to maintain their own identity and their own values against the influences and pressure of models proposed from outside.

15.  Addressing you, ladies and gentlemen, you who have been meeting in this place for over thirty years now in the name of the primacy of the cultural realities of man, human communities, peoples and nations, I say to you: with all the means at your disposal, watch over this fundamental sovereignty that every nation possesses by virtue of its own culture. Cherish it like the apple of your eye for the future of the great human family. Protect it! Do not allow this fundamental sovereignty to become the prey of some political or economic interest. Do not allow it to become a victim of totalitarian and imperialistic systems or hegemonies, for which man counts only as an object of domination and not as the subject of his own existence. For them, too, the nation—their own nation or others—counts only as an object of domination and a bait for various interests, and not as a subject: the subject of sovereignty coming from the true culture which belongs to it as its own. Are there not, on the map of Europe and the world, nations which have *a marvelous historic sovereignty* derived from their culture, and which are, nevertheless, deprived of their full sovereignty at the same

time? Is this not an important point for the future of human culture, important above all in our age, when it is so urgent to eliminate the vestiges of colonialism?

16. This sovereignty which exists and which draws its origin from the specific culture of the nation and society, from the primacy of the family in the work of education, and finally from the personal dignity of every man, must remain the fundamental criterion of the manner of dealing with the problem, an important one for humanity today, namely, that of *the media of social communication* (of the information which is bound up with them, and also of what is called "mass culture"). Since these media are "social" media of communication, they cannot be *means of domination over others,* on the part of agents of political power as well as of financial powers which impose their program and their model. They must become the means—and what an important means!—of expression of this society which uses them, and which also ensures their existence. They must take into account the real needs of this society. They must take into account the culture of the nation and its history. They must *respect the responsibility of the family in the field of education.* They must take into consideration the good of man, his dignity. They cannot be subjected to the criterion of interest, of the sensational and of immediate success but, taking into account ethical requirements, they must serve the construction of a "more human" life.

17. *Genus humanum arte et ratione vivit.* Fundamentally, it is affirmed that man is himself through truth, and becomes more himself through increasingly perfect knowledge of truth. I would like to pay tribute here, ladies and gentlemen, to all the merits of your Organization and at the same time to the commitment and to all the efforts of the states and institutions which you represent, in regard to the popularization of instruction at all grades and all levels, as regards the elimination of illiteracy, which signifies the lack of all instruction, even the most elementary, a lack which is painful not only from the point of view of the elementary culture of individuals and environments, but also from the point of view of socio-economic progress. There are distressing indications of

delay in this field, bound up with a distribution of goods that is often radically unequal and unjust; think of the situations in which there exist, alongside a plutocratic oligarchy limited in numbers, multitudes of starving citizens living in want. This delay can be eliminated not by way of bloody struggles for power, but above all by means of systematic alphabetization through the spread and popularization of instruction. An effort in this direction is necessary if it is then desired to carry out the necessary changes in the socio-economic field. Man, who "is more," thanks also to what he "has," and to what he "possesses," must know how to possess, that is, to order and administer the means he possesses, for his own good and for the common good. For this purpose, instruction is indispensable.

18. The problem of instruction has always been closely linked with the mission of the Church. In the course of the centuries, she has founded schools at all levels; she gave birth to the medieval universities in Europe: in Paris and Bologna, in Salamanca and in Heidelberg, in Krakow and in Louvain. In our age, too, she offers the same contribution wherever her activity in this field is requested and respected. Allow me to claim in this place for Catholic families the right which belongs to all families to educate their children in schools which correspond to their own view of the world, and in particular the strict right of Christian parents not to see their children subjected, in schools, to programs inspired by atheism. That is, indeed, one of the fundamental rights of man and of the family.

19. The system of education is organically connected with the system of the different orientations given to the way of practicing and popularizing science, a purpose which is served by high-level educational establishments, universities and also, in view of the present development of specialization and scientific methods, specialized institutes. These are institutions of which it would be difficult to speak without deep emotion. They are the work benches at which man's vocation to knowledge, as well as the constitutive *link* of humanity *with truth* as the aim of knowledge, become a daily reality, become, in a sense, the daily bread of so many teachers,

venerated leaders of science, and, around them, of young researchers dedicated to science and its applications, as also of the multitude of students who frequent these centers of science and knowledge.

We find ourselves here, as it were, at the highest rungs of the ladder which man has been climbing, since the beginning, towards knowledge of the reality of the world around him, and towards knowledge of the mysteries of his humanity. This historical process has reached in our age possibilities previously unknown; it has opened to human intelligence horizons hitherto unsuspected. It would be difficult to go into detail here for, on the way to knowledge, the orientations of specializations are as numerous as the development of science is rich.


## UNESCO, Meeting Point of Human Culture

20. Your organization is a place of meeting, a meeting which embraces, in its widest sense, the whole field, so essential, of human culture. This audience is therefore the very place to greet all men of science, and to pay tribute particularly to those who are present here and who have obtained for their work the highest recognition and the most eminent world distinctions. Allow me, consequently, to express also certain wishes which, I do not doubt, will reach the thought and the hearts of the members of this august assembly.

Just as we are edified in scientific work—edified and made deeply happy—by this march of the distinterested knowledge of truth which the scholar serves with greatest dedication and sometimes at the risk of his health and even his life, we must be equally concerned by everything that is in contradiction with the principles of disinterestedness and objectivity, everything that would make science an instrument to reach aims that have nothing to do with it. Yes, we must be concerned about everything that proposes and presupposes only these non-scientific aims, demanding of men of science that they should put themselves in their service without permitting them to judge and decide, in all independence of mind, the human and ethical honesty of these purposes, or threatening them with bearing the consequences when they refuse to contribute to them.

Do these non-scientific aims of which I am speaking, this problem that I am raising, need proofs or comments? You know what I am referring to; let it suffice to mention the fact that among those who were brought before the international courts, at the end of the last world war, there were also men of science. Ladies and gentlemen, I beg you to forgive me these words, but I would not be faithful to the duties of my office if I did not utter them, not in order to return to the past, but to defend the future of science and human culture; even more, to defend the future of man and the world! I think that Socrates who, in his uncommon integrity, was able to sustain that knowledge is at the same time moral virtue, would have to climb down from his certainty if he could consider the experience of our time.

## Direct Science to the Defense of Man's Life

21.  We realize it, ladies and gentlemen; the future of man and of the world is threatened, radically threatened, in spite of the intentions, certainly noble ones, of men of learning, men of science. It is threatened because the marvellous results of their researchers and their discoveries, especially in the field of the sciences of nature, have been and continue to be exploited—to the detriment of the ethical imperative—for purposes that have nothing to do with the requirements of science, and even for *purposes of destruction and death,* and that to a degree never known hitherto, causing really unimaginable damage. Whereas science is called to be in the service of man's life, it is too often a fact that it is subjected to purposes that destroy the real dignity of man and of human life. That is the case when scientific research itself is directed towards these purposes or when its results are applied to purposes contrary to the good of mankind. That happens in the field of genetic manipulations and biological experimentations as well as in that of chemical, bacteriological or nuclear armaments.

Two considerations lead me to submit particularly to your reflection the nuclear threat which is weighing upon the world today and which, if it is not staved off, could lead to the destruction of the fruits of culture, the products of civilization elaborated throughout the centuries by successive generations of men who believed in the primacy of the spirit and who did not spare either their efforts or their fatigue. The first consideration is the following. Geopolitical reasons, economic problems of world dimension, terrible incomprehension, wounded national pride, the materialism of our age and the decadence of moral values have led our world to a situation of instability, to a frail balance which runs the risk of being destroyed at any moment as a result of errors of judgment, information or interpretation.

Another consideration is added to this disquieting perspective. Can we be sure, nowadays, that the upsetting of the balance would not lead to war, and to a war that would not hesitate to have recourse to nuclear arms? Up to now it has been said that nuclear arms have constituted a force of dissuasion which has prevented a major war from breaking out, and it is probably true. But we may wonder at the same time if it will always be so. Nuclear arms, of whatever order of magnitude or of whatever type they may be, are being perfected more and more every year, and they are being added to the arsenal of a growing number of countries. How can we be sure that the use of nuclear arms, even for purposes of national defense or in limited conflicts, will not lead to *an inevitable escalation*, leading to a destruction that mankind can never envisage or accept? But it is not you, men of science and culture, that I must ask not to close your eyes to what a nuclear war can represent for the whole of humanity (cf. *Homily for the World Day of Peace*, January 1, 1980).

22. Ladies and gentlemen, the world will not be able to continue for long along this way. A conviction, which is at the same time a *moral imperative*, forces itself upon anyone who has become aware of the situation and the stake, and who is also inspired by the elementary sense of responsibilities that are incumbent on everyone: consciences must be mobilized! *The efforts of human consciences* must be increased in propor-

tion to the tension between good and evil to which men at the end of the twentieth century are subjected. *We must convince ourselves of the priority of ethics over technology, of the primacy of the person over things, of the superiority of spirit over matter* (cf. *Redemptor hominis,* no. 16). The cause of man will be served if science forms an alliance with conscience. The man of science will really help humanity if he keeps "the sense of man's transcendence over the world and of God's over man" *(Address to the Pontifical Academy of Sciences,* November 10, 1979, no. 4).

Thus, seizing the opportunity of my presence at the headquarters of UNESCO today, I, a son of humanity and Bishop of Rome, directly address you, men of science, you who are gathered here, you the highest authorities in all fields of modern science. And through you I address your colleagues and friends of all countries and all continents.

I address you in the name of this terrible threat which weighs over mankind, and, at the same time, in the name of the future and the good of humanity all over the world. I beseech you: *let us make every effort* to establish and respect the primacy of ethics, in all fields of science. Let us do our utmost particularly to preserve the human family from the horrible perspective of nuclear war!

I tackled this subject before the General Assembly of the United Nations Organization, in New York, on October 2, of last year. I am speaking about it today to you. I appeal to your intelligence and your heart, above passions, ideologies and frontiers. I appeal to all those who, through their political or economic power, would be and are often led to impose on scientists *the conditions of their work and its orientation.* Above all I appeal to every scientist individually and to the whole international scientific community.

All together you are an enormous power: the power of intelligences and consciences! Show yourselves to be more powerful than the most powerful in our modern world! Make up your mind to give proof of the most noble solidarity with mankind: the solidarity founded on the dignity of the human person. Construct peace, beginning with the foundation: *respect for all the rights of man,* those which are connected with his material and economic dimension as well as those which are connected with the spiritual and interior dimension of his existence in this world. May wisdom inspire you! May love guide you, this love which will suffocate the growing threat of hatred and destruction! Men of science, commit all your moral authority to save mankind from nuclear destruction.

23. Today I have been given the possibility of realizing *one of the deepest desires of my heart.* I have been given the possibility of penetrating, here, within the Areopagus which is that of the whole world. I have been given the possibility of saying to all, to you, members of the United Nations Educational, Scientific and Cultural Organization, to you who are working for the good and for the reconciliation of men and peoples through all fields of culture, science and information, to say to you and to cry to you from the inmost depths of my soul: Yes! The future of man depends on culture! Yes! The peace of world depends on *the primacy of the Spirit!* Yes! The peaceful future of mankind depends on *love!*

Your personal contribution, ladies and gentlemen, is important; it is vital. It lies in the *correct approach* to the problems, to the solution of which you dedicate your service.

My final word is the following: Do not stop. Continue. Continue always.

# Bibliography

Arkes, Hadley. "On the Public Funding of Abortion" in *Human Life Review*, Vol. VI, No. 1, 1980, pp. 86-107.

Ashley, Benedict. "The Use of Moral Theory by the Church" in *Human Sexuality and Personhood*, Pope John XXIII Research Center, St. Louis, 1981, pp. 223-242.

Barbour, Ian. *Myths, Models and Paradigms*, New York, Harper & Row, 1976.

Barbour, Ian. *Issues in Science and Religion*, Englewood Cliffs, N.J., Prentice Hall, 1966.

Bellah, Robert N. "New Religious Consciousness and Crisis in Modernity" in *The New Religious Consciousness*, Berkeley, University of California Press, 1976, pp. 33-52.

Bleich, J. David. "Critique on Abortion" in *Sh'ma*, a Journal of Jewish responsibility, January 10, 1975.

Bleich, J. David. "Abortion in Halackhic Literature" in *Tradition*, 10: no. 2, 1968.

Brennan, W. "The American Medical Association on Abortion" in *Medical Holocaust*, Nordland Publishing Company, 1980, p. 331.

Brungs, S.J., Robert. "Catholic Universities and the Problems Arising from Technological Advance," in *The Catholic University Facing the Ethical Problems of the Technological Society*, Paris: Cedux, 1981.

Califano, Joseph. *Governing America*, Report from the White House and Cabinet, 1981.

California, State of, Office of Legislative Counsel, Memorandum, July 7, 1972, "Right to Privacy."

Callahan, Daniel. "The Quality of Life: What Does it Mean?" in *That They May Live*, New York, Alba House, 1971, pp. 3ff.

Callahan, Daniel. "Bioethics as a Discipline" in *Hastings Center Studies 1* (1), 1973, pp. 66-73.

Connery, John. *Abortion: The Development of the Roman Catholic Perspective*, Loyola University Press, 1977.

Connery, John. "Abortion and the Duty to Preserve Life" in *Theological Studies*, Vol. 40, No. 2, June 1979, pp. 318-333.

Curren, Charles E. "Roman Catholic Social Ethics: Past, Present and Future" in *That They May Live*, New York, Alba House, 1971, pp. 87-121.

DeLubac, Henri. *The Drama of Atheistic Humanism*, London, Sheed and Ward.

*Documents of Vatican II:* ed. Abbot and Gallagher, New York, Guild Press, 1966.

*Ethical Decision Making Regarding in Vitro Fertilization*, St. Louis, Pope John XXIII Research Center, December 8, 1978.

*Ethical Evaluation of Fetal Experimentation:* ed. D. McCarthy and A. Moraczewski, St. Louis, Pope John XXIII Research Center, 1976.

Fletcher, John C. "The Fetus as Patient: Ethical Issues" in *Journal of American Medical Association*, August 1981, pp. 772-773.

Flannery, Edward H. *Anguish of the Jews*, New York, Macmillan, 1964.

Gallup Opinion Index. *Religion in America*, Princeton, N.J., American Institute of Public Opinion, 1978.

*Genetic Counseling:* The Church and the Law, ed. S. Atkinson and A. Moraczewski, St. Louis, Pope John XXIII Research Center, 1979.

Glock, Charles Y. and Stark, Rodney. *American Piety*, Berkeley, University of California Press, 1970.

Glock, Charles Y. and Bellah, Robert N. ed. *The New Religious Consciousness*, Berkeley, University of California Press, 1976.

Goodfield, June. *Playing God: Genetic Engineering and the Manipulation of Life*, New York, Random House, 1977.

Gorman, James. "Creationism vs. Evolution" in *Discover*, May 1981, pp. 32-33.

Gould, Stephen S. "In Praise of Charles Darwin" in *Discover*, February 1982, pp. 20-25.

Greeley, Andrew. *The American Catholic: A Social Portrait*, New York, Basic Books, 1977.

Greeley, Andrew; McCready, William; McCourt, K. *Catholic Schools in a Declining Church*, Kansas City, Sheed and Ward, 1976.

Haring, Bernard. *Ethics of Manipulation: Issues in Medicine, Behavior Control, and Genetics*, New York, Seabury Press, 1975.

Hellegers, Andre. "Abortion: A Help or Hindrance to Public Health" Testimony, Sub Committee United States Senate Judiciary, April 25, 1974.

Hitching, Francis. "Was Darwin Wrong About Evolution?: A Challenge by Scientists," in *Life*, April 1982.

Hoge, Dean R. *Understanding Church Growth and Decline,* New York, Pilgrim Press, 1978.

Hoge, Dean R. *Converts, Dropouts, Returnees:* Study of Religious Change Among Catholics, New York, Pilgrim Press, 1981.

Hoge, Dean R. and Hastings, Philip K. "Changes in Religion Among College Students 1948-1974" in *Journal for Scientific Study of Religion,* 15:237-49.

Hoge, Dean R. and Keeter, L. G. "Determinants of College Teachers' Religious Beliefs" in *Journal for Scientific Study of Religion,* 1976, 15 (3) 221-235.

Hook, Sidney. *From Hegel to Marx,* Ann Arbor, University of Michigan Press, 1962.

Huxley, Aldous. *Brave New World,* New York, Harper and Row, 1969.

*ITEST,* "Human Freedom in a Technological Society," St. Louis, University of St. Louis Press, April 1976.

Jaki, Stanley L. *Science and Creation,* New York, Neal Watson Academic Publications, 1974.

Jones, James. *Bad Blood, the Tuskegee Experiment,* Riverside, N.J., Free Press, 1981.

Kass, Leon R. "The New Biology: What Price Man's Estate?" in *Journal of American Medical Association,* pp. 772-3, August 14, 1981.

Kass, Leon R. "The Implications of Prenatal Diagnosis for the Human Right to Life" in *Ethical Issues in Human Genetics:* ed. Bruce Hilton, New York, Plenum Press, 1973, pp. 185-199.

Kass, Leon R. "In Vitro Fertilization: Unethical Experiments?" in *New England Journal of Medicine,* 285 (21), 1974.

Leakey, Richard E. *Origins,* New York, Dutton, 1977.

Lehman, Edward C. "Academic Discipline and Faculty Religiosity in Secular and Church Related Colleges," in *Journal for Scientific Study of Religion,* 1974.

Lepp, Ignace. *Atheism in Our Time,* New York, Macmillan, 1963.

"The Limitations of Science in the Solution of Social Issues," *Proceedings of the ITEST*—NASA Conference on the Limitations of Science in the Solution of Social Issues, March 1977, pp. 1-6.

Mandelbaum, Michael. *The Nuclear Revolution,* Cambridge University Press, 1981.

McCormick, S.J., Richard. *How Brave a New World?* New York, Doubleday and Company, 1981.

McCormick, Richard A. and Veatch, Robert. "The Preservation of Life" in *Theological Studies,* June 1980, pp. 390-396.

McCormick, Richard A. "The Preservation of Life" in *Linacre Quarterly,* Vol. 43, 1976, pp. 94-100.

McCormick, Richard A. "Notes on Moral Theology" in *Theological Studies*, Baltimore, 1977, 38:57-114; 1978, 39:76-138; 1979, 40:59-112.

*Model Penal Code*, American Law Institute, 1959.

Mohr, James C. *Abortion in America: The Origins and Evolution of a National Policy, 1800-1900*, Oxford University Press, 1978.

Moynihan, Daniel P. and Glazer, Nathan. *Beyond the Melting Pot*, Cambridge, MIT Press, 1963.

*Moral Responsibility in Prolonging Life Decisions:* ed. D. G. McCarthy and A. Moraczewski, St. Louis, Pope John XXIII Research Center, 1981.

Muggeridge, Malcolm. "The Humane Holocaust" in *The Human Life Review*, Vol. VI, No. 1, 1980.

Mulligan, J. F. and Reed, S. G. "Atomic Theory" in *New Catholic Encyclopedia*, Washington, Catholic University of America Press, Vol. 1, 1967.

Nathanson, Bernard N. *Aborting America*, New York, Doubleday, 1979.

Newton, Isaac. *Mathematical Principles of Nature Philosophy*, Berkeley, University of California Press, McGraw-Hill, 1962.

Noonan, John T. *Contraception*, Cambridge, Harvard University Press, 1965.

Noonan, John T. *A Private Choice: Abortion in America in the Seventies*, Riverside, N.J., Free Press, 1979.

O'Conner, John. "The Technologies of Warfare" in *ITEST*, St. Louis, October 1981.

O'Malley, William J. "Carl Sagan's Gospel of Scientism" in *America*, February 7, 1981, pp. 95-98.

Ong, Walter J. "Technology Outside US and Inside US" in *Communio*, V., No. 2, 1978.

Overbye, Dennis. "Is Anyone Out There?" in *Discovery*, March 1982, p. 20.

Orwell, George. *1984*, New York, New American Library, 1971.

Packard, Vance. *The Status Seekers*, New York, McKay Company.

Papal Teachings Series. *The Human Body*, Boston, St. Paul Editions, 1960.

Pope John XXIII. Encyclicals *Mater et Magistra; Pacem in Terris*, NCWC Washington, D.C., 1964.

Quay, Eugene. "Justifiable Abortion" in *Georgetown Law Review*, 49:2, 1960.

Rahner, Karl. *Do You Believe in God?* New York, Paulist Press, 1969.

Ramsey, Paul. *Fabricated Man: The Ethics of Genetic Control*, New Haven, Yale University Press, 1970.

Ramsey, Paul. *The Just War*, New York, Scribners, 1968.

Ramsey, Paul. *The Patient as Person,* New Haven, Yale University Press, 1970.

Ramsey, Paul. "The·Morality of Abortion" in *Life or Death,* University of Washington, 1968, p. 69.

Ramsey, Paul. "The Enforcement of Morals: Non-Therapeutic Research on Children" in *Hastings Center Report,* August 1976, pp. 21-30.

Ramsey, Paul. *Ethics at Edge of Life,* New Haven, Yale University Press, 1978.

Ramsey, Paul. "The Two-Step Fantastic" in *Theological Studies,* Baltimore, March 1981, pp. 122-134.

Ramsey, Paul. "Prolonged Dying: Not Medically Indicated," in *Hastings Center Report* 6, 1976, pp. 14-17.

Rathjens, George. "The Role of the Scientist in Military Preparedness" in *ITEST,* St. Louis, October 1981.

Reich, Warren T. ed. *Encyclopedia of Bioethics,* New York, Paulist Press, 1978.

Sagan, Carl. *Cosmos,* Westminster, Md., Random House, 1980.

Sagan, Carl. "The Search for Who We Are" in *Discovery,* March 1982, p. 30.

*Scientific American,* November 1976, "Effects of Atomic First Strike."

Shannon, Thomas A. "Ethical Implications of Developments in Genetics" *Linacre Quarterly,* November 1980, pp. 346-368.

Sheridan, Thomas B. "Computer Control and Human Alienation" in *Document No. 12B,* Conf. on Faith, Science and the Future, WCC, July 12-24, 1979, Cambridge, Mass.

*Sun Times,* Chicago, November 12, December 6, December special edition, "Abortion Profiteers," 1981.

*That They May Live: On Quality of Life,* ed. G. Devine, New York, Alba House, 1971.

Toffler, Alvin. *Future Shock,* Westminster, Md., Random House, 1970.

Varga, S.J., Andrew. *The Main Issues in Bioethics,* New York, Paulist Press, 1980.

Weber, Leonard. *Who Shall Live?* New York, Paulist Press, 1976.

Westin, Alan F. *Databanks in a Free Society,* Alexandria, Virginia, Time-Life Books, 1974.

Wilson, E. O. *The New Religion,* Cambridge, Harvard University Press, 1978.

World Council of Churches, *Faith and Science in an Unjust World* (2 vol.) Report of WCC Conference on Faith, Science and the Future, Montreux, Imprimerie Corbaz, 1980.

# Biography

## Bishop Mark J. Hurley

Mark Joseph Hurley was born in San Francisco in 1919. Ordained a priest in 1944, he did graduate studies at the University of California, Berkeley and at the Catholic University of America in Washington, D. C., where he received his Ph.D. degree in 1947. He received his J.C.B. degree in Canon Law at the Lateran University in Rome.

Bishop Hurley served as a teacher and subsequently principal of two high schools in California as well as assistant superintendent and superintendent of schools and as a teacher in the graduate schools of several universities. He was a peritus at the Second Vatican Council as a consulting member to the Commission on Seminaries, Universities and Schools from 1962 to 1965. He was also a regular member of the U.S.A. Press Panel during the Vatican Council.

In 1967 he was named Auxiliary Bishop of San Francisco and in 1969, Bishop of the Diocese of Santa Rosa in California. As bishop he has served as the first chairman of the U.S.A. Bishop's Committee on Science, Technology and Human Values from 1973 to 1978, and as chairman of the Social Development and World Peace Committee since 1980. He is also a Trustee of the Catholic University of America.

Among his published works are: *Church-State Relationships in Education in California; Commentary on the Declaration of Christian Education of Vatican II; Education in Peru; Curriculum in Social Studies.*

Since 1973 Bishop Hurley has served as a member of the Secretariat for Non-Believers in Rome, which addresses among its purposes the relationship of the Church and science.

# Index

# Daughters of St. Paul

IN MASSACHUSETTS
  50 St. Paul's Ave., Jamaica Plain, Boston, MA 02130;
  **617-522-8911; 617-522-0875**
  172 Tremont Street, Boston, MA 02111; **617-426-5464;**
  **617-426-4230**
IN NEW YORK
  78 Fort Place, Staten Island, NY 10301; **212-447-5071**
  59 East 43rd Street, New York, NY 10017; **212-986-7580**
  625 East 187th Street, Bronx, NY 10458; **212-584-0440**
  525 Main Street, Buffalo, NY 14203; **716-847-6044**
IN NEW JERSEY
  Hudson Mall — Route 440 and Communipaw Ave.,
  Jersey City, NJ 07304; **201-433-7740**
IN CONNECTICUT
  202 Fairfield Ave., Bridgeport, CT 06604; **203-335-9913**
IN OHIO
  2105 Ontario St. (at Prospect Ave.), Cleveland, OH 44115; **216-621-9427**
  25 E. Eighth Street, Cincinnati, OH 45202; **513-721-4838**
IN PENNSYLVANIA
  1719 Chestnut Street, Philadelphia, PA 19103; **215-568-2638**
IN VIRGINIA
  1025 King St., Alexandria, VA 22314 **703-683-1741**
IN FLORIDA
  2700 Biscayne Blvd., Miami, FL 33137; **305-573-1618**
IN LOUISIANA
  4403 Veterans Memorial Blvd., Metairie, LA 70002; **504-887-7631;**
  **504-887-0113**
  1800 South Acadian Thruway, P.O. Box 2028, Baton Rouge, LA 70821
  **504-343-4057; 504-343-3814**
IN MISSOURI
  1001 Pine Street (at North 10th), St. Louis, MO 63101; **314-621-0346;**
  **314-231-1034**
IN ILLINOIS
  172 North Michigan Ave., Chicago, IL 60601; **312-346-4228**
  **312-346-3240**
IN TEXAS
  114 Main Plaza, San Antonio, TX 78205; **512-224-8101**
IN CALIFORNIA
  1570 Fifth Avenue, San Diego, CA 92101; **714-232-1442**
  46 Geary Street, San Francisco, CA 94108; **415-781-5180**
IN HAWAII
  1143 Bishop Street, Honolulu, HI 96813; **808-521-2731**
IN ALASKA
  750 West 5th Avenue, Anchorage AK 99501; **907-272-8183**
IN CANADA
  3022 Dufferin Street, Toronto 395, Ontario, Canada
IN ENGLAND
  128, Notting Hill Gate, London W11 3QG, England
  133 Corporation Street, Birmingham B4 6PH, England
  5A-7 Royal Exchange Square, Glasgow G1 3AH, England
  82 Bold Street, Liverpool L1 4HR, England
IN AUSTRALIA
  58 Abbotsford Rd., Homebush, N.S.W., Sydney 2140, Australia